D1016425

13.⁵⁰

TRANSFORMING
POWER

Biblical Strategies for

Making a Difference

in Your Community

ROBERT C. LINTHICUM

IVP Books
An imprint of InterVarsity Press
Downers Grove, Illinois

InterVarsity Press
P.O. Box 1400, Downers Grove, IL 60515-1426
World Wide Web: www.ivpress.com
E-mail: email@ivpress.com

InterVarsity Press® is the book-publishing division of InterVarsity Christian Fellowship/USA®, a student movement active on campus at hundreds of universities, colleges and schools of nursing in the United States of America, and a member movement of the International Fellowship of Evangelical Students. For information about local and regional activities, write Public Relations Dept., InterVarsity Christian Fellowship/USA, 6400 Schroeder Rd., P.O. Box 7895, Madison, WI 53707-7895, or visit the IVCF website at <www.intervarsity.org>.

Scripture quotations, unless otherwise noted, are from the New Revised Standard Version of the Bible, copyright 1989 by the Division of Christian Education of the National Council of the Churches of Christ in the USA. Used by permission. All rights reserved.

Quotes from Donald B. Kraybill, The Upside-Down Kingdom © 1990 are used by permission of Herald Press.

Quotes from Robert C. Linthicum, City of God; City of Satan: A Biblical Theology of the Urban Church © 1991 are used by permission of the author.

Quotes from Robert C. Linthicum, "Doing Community Organizing in the Urban Slums of India," Social Policy 32, no. 2 (2001-2002): 34-38 are used by permission of the publisher.

Cover design: Cindy Kiple
Cover images: business meeting: Ryan McVay/Getty Images
             arial: Photodisc Collection/Getty Images

ISBN-10: 0-8308-3228-9
ISBN-13: 978-0-8308-3228-6

Printed in the United States of America ∞

Library of Congress Cataloging-in-Publication Data

Linthicum, Robert C.
    Transforming power: biblical strategies for making a difference in
your community / Robert C. Linthicum.
        p. cm.
Includes bibliographical references and indexes.
    ISBN 0-8308-3228-9 (pbk.: alk. paper)
    1. Power (Christian theology) 2. Sociology, Christian. I. Title.
    BT738.25.L57 2003
    261—dc21

                                                            2003010917

P	19	18	17	16	15	14	13	12	11	10	9	8	7	6	5	4	3	2
Y	21	20	19	18	17	16	15	14	13	12	11	10	09	08	07	06		

"For the kingdom of God

depends not on talk

but on power."

THE APOSTLE PAUL
(1 COR 4:20)

CONTENTS

Acknowledgments

THE THEOLOGY AND PRACTICE OF relational power as presented in this book is not something I have developed on my own. What I know and what I practice have not come simply from my own research and ministry experiences but from working with people who use power effectively. I have been doing biblical research around a theology of power since 1961, and I am indebted to scholars like Walter Brueggemann, Donald Kraybill, André Trocmé, Walter Wink and a host of other biblical scholars and practitioners who have enriched my personal study.

In the concrete practice of relational power, I have had four "fathers" who have helped to mold my practice of power at different stages of my ministry. These four, for whom I am deeply grateful, are the Reverend Charles Jordan (an African American pastor and professional organizer who introduced me to and discipled me in community organizing in Rockford, Illinois, from 1967 to 1969), Robert Linn (who mentored and trained me in organizing in Chicago from 1970 through 1975), Mike Miller (who both encouraged my biblical research and honed my skills between 1987 and 1998) and Ernesto Cortes Jr. (who has inspired and challenged me since 1998 as I have worked under his guidance in the Los Angeles Metropolitan Organizing Strategy). If these are my fathers in organizing, then my grandfather would be Saul David Alinsky, whose precedent-shattering work of equipping "ordinary folk" to be significantly engaged in public life reshaped cities in the United States between 1938 and 1972.

There are many others, as well, who have contributed both to my pursuit of the theological task and the honing of my skills in community organizing.

I'm indebted to people like Marilyn Stranske, John Caulkins, Rebecca Gifford, Judy Donovan, Mike Clements, Ken Fujimoto, Doug Edwards, Frank Alton, Holly Holcomb, Tom Dietrich, Joyce Manson, Leon Fanniel, Larry Gordon, Stan and Nancy Moore, Phil Tom, Tim Tseng, Wally Tilleman, Stephen Mott and many, many others.

When I headed the Office of Urban Advance for World Vision International from 1985 through 1995, I was privileged to work with community organizers, mission executives and urban pastors around the world, and there were a number who particularly pressed me toward a more theologically consistent and strategically effective exercise of relational power. To the following I owe a great deal: the Reverend Kenneth Luscombe (Australia), Dr. Stephen Githumbi (Kenya), Franklin Joseph (India), Sir Michael Eastman (Great Britain), Ruben Medina (Mexico), the Reverend David Ashiko (Kenya), Dr. Sam Kamaleson (India), Dr. Osborne Joda-Mbewe (Malawi), Dr. Bryant Myers (U.S.A.), the Reverend Darci Dusilek (Brazil), Father Benigno Beltran (Philippines), Lawrence Mangalarajan (India), Remedios Geraldes (Philippines), Bwalya Melu (Zambia), Father Alfonso Navarro (Mexico), the Reverend Max Chigwida (Zimbabwe), Father Leo Penta (Italy), Paul Abbott (Mauritania), Charles Clayton (U.K.) and Philip Hunt (Australia).

Finally, my deepest appreciation and gratitude go to my best friend, closest companion, lover and wife, Marlene, who for more than forty years has been willing to share me with the church and the cause of justice, and who has been my prayer warrior, advocate, encourager and best critic. For all these brothers and sisters, I praise the Lord!

INTRODUCTION

"BOB, I HAVE A REQUEST TO MAKE OF YOU," a business friend of mine said recently.

"What's that, Richard?"

"I have grown sick and tired of all the political intrigue that goes on in my business. It seems that every company I've worked for has constant power plays, and I'm tired of coping with it all day long. I think I would like to work for some Christian ministry or church, and not have to cope with the use of power all the time."

I must confess that I burst out in laughter. It wasn't a nice thing to do, but it happened before I could think of how he might react. I just couldn't help myself. The thought of *any* ministry or church not engaging in power plays was too ridiculous for me to bear. I had to confess to Richard that I could not recommend to him any Christian mission or church organization that didn't play politics.

CHRISTIANS AND POWER

Most Christians have a problem with power; it has long had a bad name in Christian circles. There is a reason for that. Most Christian leaders are suspicious of power. They have been taught that Jesus was a loving, gentle and mild person. (We will discover in this book that he was loving; yet he was also a person who thoroughly understood power as a positive good and used it to oppose the power elite of his nation and to build a community.)

So Christian leaders see power as inconsistent with behavior that is loving, gentle and mild. They have come to that conclusion because they have experienced the abuse of power in their own ministries as it has been used to manage people, control situations, gain the desired responses and dominate the church.

It is true that power has its dark side. But it also has its bright side. Power has the potential to either be very ruthless and destructive (unilateral or dominating power) or very strengthening and liberating (relational power). Therefore understanding power and knowing how to use it to set people free and to give them purpose, direction and joy is crucial.

Power is always present in all human situations, because power is nothing more than the ability, capacity and willingness of a person, a group of people or an institution (whether it is a church or a nation) to act. The ability, capacity and willingness to act is, in itself, neither good nor bad. What makes power constructive or destructive is how it is used and for what purpose it is used (that is, whether it is designed to control and dominate people or to enable people to be in charge of their own destinies).

Therefore it is important for Christians who are involved in any kind of ministry to have an articulated and acted-out theology of power. To be legitimate, such a theology must understand power from within a biblical framework. But it must also be implemented in the everyday life of doing ministry—a use of power that is understood, is consistent with the biblical witness and is actualized in the way we do ministry. Power that can be openly acknowledged and understood can enhance the relationships between people, define and deliver on issues of common importance, facilitate the implementation of justice in the world, and build a more loving and powerful community of faith.

The first section of *Transforming Power* outlines a thorough biblical theology of power. The second part of the book gives equal time to the development and implementation of key strategies of relational power, as informed by the discipline of community and broad-based organizing.

The first part, "A Theology of Power," builds the biblical framework for acting powerfully for the common good. Chapter one articulates God's design for human society around the theme of shalom. Chapter two presents a biblical analysis of human society moving toward the oppression, exploitation and domination of its people—the very opposite of what God intends. Chapter three explores the ministry and theology of Jesus, as contained in the four Gospels, for an understanding of Jesus' commitment to shalom ("the kingdom of God"), and his actualizing it through the use of relational power to defeat the dominating power of the systems. Chapter four examines the full work of the church, including the necessity for the church to be willing to use power intelligently to work for the transformation of its society into God's design. Chapter five examines in detail a biblical use of relational power that transformed a specific society. The final chapter in this section explores the extremely mature theology of power held by the apostle Paul; his theology serves as a vehicle for synthesizing the study of power conducted thus far in the book.

The second part of this book, "The Practice of Power," examines biblical principles and strategies for exercising relational power that leads to the transformation of one's community or city. Chapter seven teaches the importance of individual meetings (one-on-ones) as the primary base for creating change. Chapter eight demonstrates how to move from individual meetings to mass actions that are designed to get a positive response from "the principalities and powers." Chapter nine examines five basic strategies for using power that are found throughout Scripture but tend to be avoided by the church today—thus significantly limiting the impact of the church on our society. Chapter ten integrates the previously explored material by examining the spirituality of relational power in its capacity to create community, to be a vehicle for sharing faith and to contribute in the formation of a shalom society—the kingdom of God.

Who should read this book? Quite simply, any Christian who wants to make a difference! It is written for anyone who has a "fire in the belly"—any Christian who is really concerned about the direction in which society is now moving and who wants to call it back to the biblical ideal. You can't hope to do that without using power—the relational power taught and practiced by God's people in the Scriptures, empowered by the work of the Holy Spirit in and through them.

You may be a pastor or a layperson, an urban church worker or a missiologist with a Ph.D., an "ordinary Joe," or a mover and shaker within your world. Whoever you are, you can't hope to bring about systemic change if you don't know how to use power. I have not created the principles and strategies of relational power taught in this book. They have been used in broad-based and community organizing by hundreds of thousands of God's people over the past sixty years, in places ranging from urban squatter settlements in Blantyre, Malawi, and Khulna, Bangladesh, to enclaves of the privileged in Grosse Pointe, Michigan, to beaches full of suntanned Southern Californians. These are tested strategies that work. But the church has done a poor job of grounding these strategies in its theology, and therefore we have tended to separate our action from our belief. This book is designed to teach you how to use relational power to make a difference in your society. But it is even more intentionally designed to ground that power in the biblical witness. For, as Paul so eloquently put it, "The kingdom of God depends not on talk but on power" (1 Cor 4:20).

Part One

A Theology
of Power

1

SOCIETY AS GOD
INTENDED IT TO BE

MY FINAL PASTORAL CHARGE BEFORE retirement was also my most thrilling. That ministry was as director of the Hollywood-Wilshire Cluster of Churches. The Cluster was an effort of churches and mission agencies in one community of Los Angeles to work together for the social transformation and evangelization of that community. I served as its director for five years, from 1995 through 1999.

Hollywood-Wilshire is a four-square-mile community in inner-city Los Angeles that has grown in population from 320,275 in 1980 to its present 435,211. That makes this geographically small community a "city" of larger population than Pittsburgh or Albuquerque or Omaha or Sacramento; it is a medium-sized city in the heart of giant Los Angeles.

If anything can be said of Hollywood-Wilshire, it is that it is culturally diverse. It is 53.1 percent Hispanic, 22 percent Asian, 7.9 percent African and African American, and 17 percent Anglo. Hollywood-Wilshire includes within its borders Los Angeles's largest Central American population, America's largest Ethiopian population and the largest Korean "city" outside Korea.

The community is young: 59.4 percent are under thirty-five, while only 14 percent are over fifty-five (the national average is 26 percent). They are primarily single: 42.8 percent of the residents over eighteen are not married. More than 67 percent never attend church.

The community is both very rich and very poor—and not much in between. It contains two thriving industries: the entertainment industry centered in Hollywood and the financial industry of Los Angeles, which is in Wilshire. Movie moguls, financiers and even the mayor of Los Angeles all live within its borders. And forty thousand primarily Anglo and Korean people commute by public transportation every day to work in Wilshire's high-rise towers.

But Hollywood-Wilshire is also very, very poor. Eighty-two percent of the people live in rental units, have hourly-rate or blue-collar jobs, are unemployed, or work within the "informal sector" (translated: they are undocumented workers in the United States without the permission of the U.S. government, carrying fake or no Social Security cards, and working at slave wages and under abominable working conditions, or having to "make work" for themselves with small illegal operations). That 82 percent own no cars, live in substandard rental properties that are costing them one thousand dollars a month and speak a language other than English as their mother tongue.[1]

It was to deal with this "middle-sized city" in the heart of Los Angeles that churches in Hollywood and Wilshire came together to form the Cluster, aware that the problems the community and its churches faced were so overwhelming and complex that none of the churches could even "commence to start to begin" to make any kind of difference.

The churches themselves were an unusual mixture of congregations reflecting the community they sought to reach. One church was a first-generation Korean congregation, another was the oldest Formosan church in Los Angeles, a third was a Hispanic congregation, and a fourth was a neighborhood church equally divided between Filipinos and Anglos. Two were "tall steeple" churches, each at one time the largest church in its denomination but now smaller and more diverse. One of these two churches holds four worship services each Sunday, one each in English, Spanish, Korean and Amharic, the official language of Ethiopia; the other holds Sunday worship in English and in Spanish.

During the time I worked with the Cluster, it expanded from one to eight programming staff, including a lead community organizer, who was Salvadoran, and two neighborhood organizers and four youth ministry specialists, who were Korean, Chinese, Hispanic and Anglo. During those five years, we undertook shared ministries with the churches and mission agencies in community organizing, economic development, youth outreach and cross cultural evangelism. We also worked to build up the interior life of the churches and agencies through discipleship training, spiritual formation and fundraising.

It's hard to summarize five years of work by eight dedicated staff, six churches and three agencies. But here are just a few of our community ministries: community and church members were organized around their fear of crime and gangs; this involved more than 150 residents and radically reduced crime in the community. The community stopped an effort by the City of Los Angeles to approve a comprehensive plan for the community (without consulting its residents) that would have ignored the ethnic poverty in the community in favor of major business interests. More than two hundred undocumented residents completed classes in English and citizenship and made successful applications for citizenship. Partners in Community Economics was born, in which church business people mentored community residents in the start-up and development of small businesses, with loans negotiated with local Korean banks.

Youth work through four of the churches and one of the mission agencies reached several hundred gospel-resistant Korean, Taiwanese, Chinese, Filipino, African American and Hispanic youth for Christ. An average of eight hundred children and youth were involved weekly in art, sports and computer training through the HOLA (Heart of Los Angeles) program. Mainland Chinese students were reached through friendship evangelism at the nearby University of Southern California and UCLA campuses. Eight postcollege men and women each year worked full time in hands-on urban ministry to the largely Hispanic South Hollywood community while being trained in urban ministry. Churches organized their members and community residents around the issues of immigration, citizenship, employment and income generation. Thus the Cluster and its churches and agencies began to "make a dent" in this community.

Through the Cluster, these churches, their pastors and their people learned to act powerfully. And they learned to act powerfully by acting together. This is just one example of what can happen when Christians learn to use power to bring about transformation. As God's people, we are far more powerful than we think we are. We can make a profound difference in our neighborhoods, communities and cities—far greater than we believe we can.

But in order to accomplish change, we have to learn how to use power. And as Christians, we must learn how to use power in a Christian manner—relationally, not unilaterally—because relational power is of the essence of the gospel. That is what the churches and mission agencies of the Hollywood-Wilshire Cluster discovered. And that is what I have discovered over my forty-six years of ministry in the United States and in Africa, Asia and Latin America. How to understand and use biblical power is what this book is about.

POWER MISUSED

But I haven't always known how to use transforming power. As a young man in ministry, I was hopelessly naive. For example, in 1957, while I was a college student, I was working among African American teenagers in a government housing project in a U.S. city. This housing project was built to warehouse the poor in high-rise buildings of poor construction and design. Our ministry among those youth included recreational and athletic activities that were designed to open them to hearing the gospel. Once they received Christ, they were encouraged to join our Bible studies, where they would be discipled and connected to the life of a local church.

One of the youth who began to actively participate in our Bible studies was a new Christian named Eva. She was an exceptionally beautiful teenager, physically mature for her age. Eva became even more radiant when she received Christ as her Lord and Savior. I began discipling her, building her up in the "nurture and admonition" of the Lord.

My academic year was drawing to a close, and I was looking forward to returning home for summer vacation. Just before I was to leave my teenage "parish," however, Eva came to me greatly troubled. "Bob," she said, "I am under terrible pressure and I don't know what to do about it. There is a very powerful gang of men in this project that recruits girls to be prostitutes. They are trying to force me to join them. I know it's wrong, but what should I do about it?"

I didn't know what to say to Eva. Nothing in my experience had prepared me to deal with something like this. After all, I was only a nineteen-year-old, middle-class white boy! The only thing I could think to do was to share with her what I had learned in Sunday school and in the Christian college I attended—to "resist evil and it will flee from you," to "commit your way unto the Lord and he will give you the desires of your heart." I urged her to stick with her Bible study group and not to give in to the gang's demands.

And then I left for my summer vacation.

Three months later, I returned to college and to that ministry. Eva had stopped attending the Bible study. When I asked about her, the other youth told me she had stopped coming about a month after I had left. I feared the worst! I went to Eva's apartment in one of the project buildings to talk with her. When she answered the door and saw that it was me, she burst into tears. "They got to me, Bob," she said. "I'm one of their whores!"

"Eva, how could you give in?" I unsympathetically responded. "Why didn't you resist?"

"I did resist!" she replied. "I didn't give in; I was forced in." Then she told me a story of sheer intimidation and terror. "First, they told me they would beat my father if I didn't become one of their whores. I refused—and they beat him bad. Then they said my brother was next. I still refused, and he ended up in the hospital with both legs broken. Then they told me that if I didn't yield, they would gang rape my mother. I knew they meant it, and I couldn't allow that. So I gave in."

"But Eva," I said, "why did you let them intimidate you that way? Why didn't you get some protection? Why didn't you go to the police?"

"Bob, you honkey," Eva responded in disgust, "who do you think the gang is?"

Suddenly it hit me. This gang of "very powerful men" Eva was describing was the police. The police—the very people entrusted with the task of protecting and defending the people—were in reality the real exploiters and oppressors of the people, for they were the gang operating the prostitution ring and recruiting young girls like Eva out of that slum. Here was evil like I had never known it before. And later it was discovered that this was not simply a single police precinct gone astray. What was happening in that one precinct was the tip of the iceberg in what was a city-wide operation of gambling, prostitution, and drug and bootleg liquor distribution by the police, with the judiciary organized to legally protect from exposure and prosecution this betrayal of the people.[2]

It was in this encounter in 1957 that I discovered two things. First, I realized that the power of the world's evil is far greater than the sins of its individuals. The very systems of a city or nation can become corrupt, grasping, oppressive and exploitive. And it mattered little even if all the Evas among that nation's poor were to be won to Christ as long as the evil in the systems could be allowed to run unchecked and destroy these Evas.

Second, I realized that my theology was inadequate for ministry in that kind of evil-powered world. Through Eva's tragedy I realized that if the church does not deal with the systems and structures of evil, it will not be effective in transforming the lives of that city's individuals. What I needed, I realized, was a biblical theology that would be equal to the challenge of the social *and* individual sin of the world.

In this book I seek to present a theology and practice of power that is transformative. But one cannot posit a theology of power unless one first understands how the political, economic and religious systems of a society function, because it is those systems that will use power in either destructive or constructive ways. And we, as God's people, will either have to confront the abuse of power or affirm its use. Therefore we must begin our theological reflection on power by grasping the biblical message on the systems of society.

The Scriptures present both a vision of the world as God intends it to be and a brutally frank analysis of the world as it is. Most of the writers of the Bible were motivated by a perception of God's intentions for human society—not only spiritual, but also economic, political and social. The Bible paints a very clear picture of the way society is meant to be and a vision of the world toward which we should be powerfully working.

But the Scriptures also present a brutally frank analysis of what causes our world to go awry. That analysis is articulated by Israel's prophets; given example in the actions and policies of Israel's kings, high priests and leaders; experienced by God's people under the brutality of many empires; and reflected even in the policies and actions of the Israelite priesthood and the church itself. Allowing the Scriptures to inform our personal and corporate understanding of human society helps us understand the misuse of power, enabling us to make sense of the world we experience today.

In this chapter we will examine the biblical vision of the world as God sought it to be through Israel and the church. In the next chapter we'll explore the biblical writers' understanding of what keeps going wrong.

THE SYSTEMS OF SOCIETY

A standard sociological technique for understanding the corporate life of any social unit—a family, a church, an institution, a city or a nation—is to understand it as three intertwined and integrated systems. If we are to perceive the depth of the social analysis that is occurring in Scripture as it describes the world as God intended it to be and the world as it actually is, we need to first understand clearly what systems are and how they act.

First, there is the *political system,* that system by which society makes decisions about its common life. Politics is simply the agreed-upon means by which society orders its life through the making of public and private decisions. The essential question of the political system is, how do we as a people determine to live together?

Second, the *economic system* is that agreed-upon means by which a society's goods and services are generated and distributed. For all its complexity, economics is profoundly simple at its heart; it simply has to do with the way society agrees to generate and apportion wealth. The essential question of the economic system is, how do we as a people choose to create and distribute our wealth?

Third, the *religious system* is a little more complex—not because the system itself is complex, but because of the predetermined meanings we bring to the word *religion.* The Latin root for the English *religion* simply means "that which fences about." In other words, what one believes sets the parameters around one's life. Our "religion," therefore, is the system which inculcates in a society the essential beliefs, values and basic convictions on which that society constructs its life together. The essential question of the religious system is, what do we, as a people, ultimately value?

Core values and the organizing of a society. Of the three systems, the most strategic is the religious system. If we were to describe the systems as a triangle, "religion" would have to be placed at the apex of the triangle, while "politics" and "economics" would occupy the two base angles. What a society *believes* will radically shape how that society chooses to order its corporate life and distribute its resources—not the other way around!

For example, the core value of American society is encapsulated in the words of the Declaration of Independence: "We hold these truths to be self-evident, that all [people] are created equal, that they are endowed by their Creator with certain unalienable Rights, that among these are Life, Liberty and the pursuit of Happiness." That value, translated into the political ordering of the United States, required a system that would guarantee that all people are treated equally by instituting "one man, one vote" and thus dictated an elected, representative form of government. Nothing else would have been acceptable to the populace. That core value also required an economic system of private entrepreneurship in which each person or family could be free to produce their own goods and exchange the same for the goods produced by others through the medium of money.

Every unit of society is organized through its religious, political and economic systems. A family has recognized ways that decisions are made and policies are established regarding the distribution of goods and services. The same is true of a church, a school, a formal or informal gathering of people, a corporation, a college, a city or even a nation. All units of society make decisions together regarding the ordering of their life and the distribution of their wealth based on the values they espouse as a people or group.

What is a system? We have used the word *system* to describe the political, economic and value-creating functions of society. Exactly what do we mean by *system?* A system is an organized body of people gathered together around three components: *values* that are held in common, *structures* that institutionalize those values, and *individuals* who manage and operate those institutions. All three components must exist for a system to be a system. Let's look at them more closely.

Values, beliefs and convictions (that is, a system's or society's "religion") form the core of a system. Those values are both *articulated* and *unarticulated.* Articulated values are those to which the populace of a system gives clear recognition (for example, "one man, one vote"). The unarticulated values are those beliefs and convictions that are rarely given voice but serve as operating assumptions for those who hold considerable power in the system ("power or money increases your influence"). Often the unarticulated values oppose the articulated values, and because they are unarticulated and are held by those with the most power, they are usually more powerful than the articulated values—even though those in power will give lip service to the articulated values. This was one of the chief criticisms Jesus had of the Pharisees (see, for example, Mt 23:3). These religious leaders talked about the importance of obedience to the law but were actually using the law to bring both wealth and power to themselves.

Structures are the means by which the articulated values are institutionalized in that society and are thus lived out. Values, by themselves, will have no shaping effect on a society unless structures are devised to implement and carry out those values in the life of that society. Structures are necessary for the values to be practiced effectively. Thus "no taxation without representation" was a core idea around which the Revolutionary War was fought. But it was only an idea until it was concretized in a structure that adequately carried out the core values and principles of the United States: a federal government consisting of three bodies—the legislative, the executive and the judicial.

Individuals are those who people the structure and thus manage and operate institutions. Without people who make the structures work, the institutions are empty vessels incapable of implementing the core values of a society. The strong unification of the United States capable of withstanding the triple onslaught of slavery, the Civil War and the growth of giant corporations—was due to the rising to power in each of the three branches of government of several people of immense vision, power and determination: Chief Justice John Marshall in the judiciary, John Quincy Adams and Andrew Jackson in the presidency, and Daniel Webster in the legislature. Without these four men working to preserve the Union against the drive for states' rights, secession and slavery, the Constitution would have been dissolved and the United States would have ceased to exist.

Thus all three—values, structures and individuals—are necessary for the creation and sustenance of a system. When we talk about *systemic change,* therefore, we recognize that significant change cannot occur in a society unless the articulated values of that society are truly embraced, and that cannot occur unless structures function to implement those values and unless individuals who run those structures work for the interests of the people. *Only when individuals and structures and values change, do you have systemic change.*

Community organizers are fond of speaking of the world as it is and the world as it should be. They rightly insist that we can't really make a difference in our church, city or world unless we have a vision of both. What we will do for the remainder of this chapter is seek to discern what the Bible teaches about the world as God intended it to be.

THE WORLD AS IT SHOULD BE (ACCORDING TO DEUTERONOMY)

The book of Deuteronomy is the clearest statement in the Bible of the world as God intended it to be. The word *Deuteronomy* means "the second telling of the Law"; this book presents a summarization or retelling of the law, a systematic presentation of what is otherwise somewhat haphazardly fashioned throughout Exodus, Numbers and Leviticus. Deuteronomy is the closest Israel ever came to the development of a constitution, laying out what one nation under God ought to look like.

The author of 2 Kings tells us that King Josiah repented when he heard Deuteronomy read, because he realized how far his kingdom had departed from God's ideal (2 Kings 22:3-20). Deuteronomy brought about the reforms recorded in 2 Kings 22—23, which sought to rescue Judah from almost certain annihilation by the world powers. Deuteronomy formed the foundation for the rebuilding of the walls of Jerusalem and the reformulation of the corporate life of Israel under Nehemiah. Deuteronomy formed the template for the nation against which the prophets measured Israel. Deuteronomy, along with the book of Isaiah, was most used by Jesus to call Israel to accountability. And Deuteronomy formed the base for John's vision of the New Jerusalem.

As we study Deuteronomy, it is very important that we allow the Bible to speak for itself. Our natural tendency is to read a specific Scripture text in light of the present political, economic and religious environment rather than to allow the Scripture to critique the environment. Thus, for example, rather than living with the tension of the sabbatical year stipulation that all debts are to be forgiven every seven years (Deut 15:1-2) and honestly asking, "How can we live out this stipulation as Christians in today's world?" we choose to ignore the injunction by saying, "That stipulation would never work in a capitalist economy." In other words, we are using today's economic environment as the means by which we determine which portion of Scripture we will take seriously and which we will summarily dismiss.

That is a very dangerous way to read Scripture. It is to misread and thus misuse Scripture (what is called in the formal study of the Scripture, "eisegesis" rather than "exegesis"). In essence our task, as we work with the Bible, is to allow Scripture to read us rather than us to read it.

We must move through three steps when reading Scripture. First, we must discern that Scripture's *context:* to whom was it written, and what was going on at the time that would be impacting those people—especially what was happening politically, economically and religiously in that society? Second, we must perceive that Scripture's *message:* what was it saying to the people for whom it was written that would enable them to more effectively understand and cope with their world? Third, we must listen to that Scripture's *application:* in light of the message the writer was seeking to communicate to the people, what is it saying to us? Only in this way are we allowing Scripture to read us and to truly become God's Word to our situation today.

What happens if we apply the principles of biblical exegesis presented above to the book of Deuteronomy? We will discover that Deuteronomy presents God's design for the way the political, economic and religious systems of Israel are meant to operate. Following is a summary of that description.

A religion of relationship. When Jesus asked the lawyer to summarize the law, the man's reply was this: "You shall love the Lord your God with all your heart, and with all your soul, and with all your strength, and with all your mind; and your neighbor as yourself." Jesus commended him: "You have given the right answer; do this, and you will live" (Lk 10:27-28).

The first segment of the young man's summary of the law—the love of God—was the quoting of Deuteronomy 6:5; the second segment—the love of neighbor—was from Leviticus 19:18. But although Leviticus states that second commandment in the most pithy way, the perspective that one must love the neighbor and God runs throughout the book of Deuteronomy.

The basic reality of Israelite life, according to Deuteronomy, is that of being centered in a national relationship with God.

So now, O Israel, what does the LORD your God require of you? Only to fear the LORD your God, to walk in all his ways, to love him, to serve the LORD your God with all your heart and with all your soul, and to keep the commandments of the LORD your God and his decrees that I am commanding you today, for your own well-being. . . . For the LORD your God is God of gods and Lord of lords, the great God, mighty and awesome, who is not partial and takes no bribe, who executes justice for the orphan and the widow, and who loves the strangers, providing them food and clothing. You shall also love the stranger, for you were strangers in the land of Egypt. You shall fear the LORD your God; him alone you shall worship; to him you shall hold fast, and by his name you shall swear. (Deut 10:12-13, 17-20)

This passage captures in the most beautiful and compelling language the primary emphasis throughout Deuteronomy. Israel is to be centered in Yahweh. The God of Abraham and Sarah, of Isaac and Rebecca, of Moses and Zipporah is to become their God too. And that is to happen both at a national level and at a personal level.

Israel is to be in a national love relationship with God: "Hear, O Israel: The LORD is our God, the LORD alone. You shall love the LORD your God with all your heart" (Deut 6:4-5, emphasis mine). This is not a command simply to individuals. This is a command to a *nation*. But how can a nation love God?

The foundation for Israel's national life is what today would be called a *relational culture*. A relational culture is one in which power is shared through the people's participation both in the formation and in the ongoing functioning of their society's political, economic and religious (values-sustaining) systems. Relational power—or people power—seeks to distribute power, with public life built around the relationships people have with one another, including those in authority. Such a culture was very evident in Israel's early years when the social structure was "flat," with any Israelite having direct access to each leader. Such a relational culture is clearly assumed by the author of Deuteronomy as a precondition for the successful exercise of power.

The foundation of Israelite culture was both social and personal relationship with God. A relationship with God had both a public dimension and a private (or personal) dimension. Nothing is as important as our individual and our societal relationship with God and with each other. The author is not interested in the nation or its people simply holding right beliefs about

God, embracing right doctrines or celebrating right liturgies. What Deuteronomy wants is an active, dynamic relationship with God on the part of the nation—of all its people and of each person. In the final analysis, Israel's capacity to be the kind of society God desires and calls it to be depends upon the Israelites' capacity to respond to God's love with like love.

The premise of Deuteronomy is that if the nation and its people are in love with God, it will inevitably be a nation that loves its people. And why? Simply because God is in love with the people: "[God] loves the strangers, providing them food and clothing. You shall also love the stranger, for you were strangers in the land of Egypt" (Deut 10:18-19). A culture that places its primary value on relationship to God must also be a culture that places primary value on people and their well-being. So the Deuteronomic intention to build a society on a love relationship with God and each other must inevitably move that society to shape its political system in conformity to those love relationships.

Such a relational culture is commanded by Deuteronomy to be extended to "strangers" (Deut 10:19) and "aliens within your gates" but not to "foreigners" or "many nations" (Deut 15:3-6). The differentiation is important. The "stranger" or "alien" was a person of another ethnic or racial group or of another nation who had surrendered belief in his or her god and embraced Yahweh (for example, Ruth; see Ruth 1:16-17). The "foreigner" or people of "many nations" were those either inside or outside Israel who embraced the gods of unilateral aristocratic or military power (Amon-Re, Baal), or rapaciousness or concupiscence (Dagon, Ashteroth).[3]

Thus Israel is enjoined by Deuteronomy to have nothing to do with nations or peoples who ran their societies through a conspiracy of kings, economic elite, priests and the military for the purpose of dominating the people and using them as serfs. This injunction is not because of racial, ethnic or national discrimination. It is because Israel stands for a national justice and relational culture that is opposed to what the other nations stand for. And if Israel does not keep itself separate from those nations, it will eventually be seduced by those nations into forming a society equally committed to domination by the wealthy and powerful and devoid of a people truly right with God and each other.

A politics of justice. Deuteronomy names two systems for ordering the political life of Israel: the judicial system and the system of governance (that is, the king). What Deuteronomy presents regarding the judicial system is remarkable for its time. The role of *the judge* in Israelite life is laid out as follows: "You must not distort justice; you must not show partiality; and you must not accept bribes, for a bribe blinds the eyes of the wise and subverts the cause of those who are in the right. Justice, and only justice, you shall pursue, so that you may live and occupy the land that the LORD your God is giving you" (Deut 16:19-20).

The responsibility of the judicial system is to mete out justice according to the law. Judges are not to be influenced by the rank or position of the person before them for judgment; they are not to accept bribes, because that will subvert justice. To guarantee that justice will indeed occur, Deuteronomy creates an appellate court system. If a judge feels he cannot adjudicate a case after hearing it, or if a person feels she has received biased treatment from the judge, that person has the right to appeal that case to a higher court (Deut 17:8-13). And the judgment of that higher court, adjudicated not by secular judges but by the Levitical priests (who are presumably more sensitive to the leading and prompting of God) is to be final (Deut 17:12).

Deuteronomy is the book that first presents the office of *the king* to Israel (the second of the two political systems of the nation). In essence, Deuteronomy significantly limits the rights and privileges of the king of Israel so that he is reduced to a vice regent under the true king, Yahweh (Deut 17:14-20). In all nations other than Israel, the king was an absolute monarch, the sole voice of authority in the land. There was no other authority but his, because he was a total despot. The judiciary was an instrument of the king, adjudicating the laws he himself had set. The bureaucracy existed to implement the decisions of the king.

The king was allowed such power by nobles and common people alike because he was seen as the incarnation (in Egypt) or manifestation (in Assyria and Babylonia) of that nation's chief god; he was their god "enfleshed." The king controlled not only the political and religious life of the nation but also its economic system. He operated under the assumption that all the wealth of the land belonged to him. Therefore the king was, in his single person, the religious, political and economic systems personified.

Israelite kingship, as defined by Deuteronomy, was profoundly different.

The king was to be a commoner, an ordinary person whom God would select to be monarch. His reign could not be passed on to his heirs. Rather, each new monarch would be chosen from the people. The reward of the Israelite king for wisely ruling his nation was not to accumulate wealth for himself or his family or tribe. He was to live frugally. He was not to have a harem or many wives. He was not to enslave his subjects or sell them into slavery to another king. Finally, he was to keep a copy of the book of the Law before him and have a portion of it read each day to him in order to remind himself of his obligations as a king (not his privileges). Kingship, as described in Deuteronomy, was unlike any monarchy existing anywhere else in the East.

Deuteronomy communicated to those in the political system that the system exists to dispense justice. The judiciary is clearly ordered and is separated from the authority of the king. For the monarch, justice is the inevitable result of rulership that exists to serve the people, and he is not to perceive the nation as his personal property for him to use to further his own ends or to increase his wealth. A nation and culture built on relationship with God and each other requires a government that will seek justice in all it does.

An economics of equality. A nation and culture built on relationship with God and a politics of justice for all in the realm must inevitably deal with how wealth is generated and distributed. So Deuteronomy presents the economic profile of a nation truly under God. Deuteronomy reminds the Israelites that Palestine existed, with all its wealth and power, before they were born and before they entered the land (Deut 6:10). He reminds them that it was God who took them out of Egypt "with a strong hand and a mighty arm," it was God who rescued them from slavery, it was God who protected them in the desert for forty years and there molded them into a mighty nation, and it was God who brought them into the Promised Land and gave to them all of its wealth. "[You live, Israel, in] fine, large cities *that you did not build,* houses . . . *that you did not fill,* hewn cisterns *that you did not hew,* vineyards and olive groves *that you did not plant"* (Deut 6:10-11, emphasis mine).

In other words, Deuteronomy is reminding Israel that all that they have is a gift from God. Israel has not pulled itself up by its own bootstraps! The wealth the nation possesses is a free gift from God, a wealth that God has chosen to invest in them. And why? God has chosen them simply out of love for them. And why does God love them? Not because there is something about them that is so good that they are commended to God. God has chosen to love them because they were beaten down and enslaved and powerless (Deut 7:1-13)—and God is always on the side of the powerless or marginalized.

What then does God expect of them? God expects that they will use this wealth they have been given for the benefit of all the people (Deut 6—8). This wealth does not belong to them. It is a gift from God. Therefore they are to perceive it not as a private wealth to be owned but *as a common wealth* that God has invested in them so they can be good trustees or stewards of it. The nation must keep before them the recognition that all that they have is a gift. Since it belongs to God and is only temporarily invested in God's people, they are to use it for the common good by being wise trustees of it.

For what purpose are they to manage this wealth? Here Deuteronomy presents its most radical insight—as radical for its time as it is for our own. Wealth is given to the nation to be used for one purpose only: "There will, however, be no one in need among you, because the LORD is sure to bless you in the land that the LORD your God is giving you as a possession to occupy, if only you will obey the LORD your God by diligently observing this entire commandment that I command you today" (Deut 15:4-5).

Deuteronomy 15 actually states three things about poverty. First, poverty is wrong and should be eliminated from God's nation (Deut 15:4). Second, the fact is that no matter how you work to eliminate poverty, "there will never cease to be some in need on the earth" (Deut 15:11). Therefore, third, "I . . . command you, 'Open your hand to the poor and needy neighbor in your land'" (Deut 15:11). Everyone in the nation is to work for the eradication of poverty by the way the people and the systems manage their wealth. The elimination of poverty in the nation is to be the primary agenda both of the systems and of each individual Israelite.[4]

Deuteronomy is replete with instructions as to how the nation can guarantee that the economy is managed in such a way that poverty will be eliminated. One such way is to observe *the sabbatical year*: "Every seventh year you shall grant a remission of debts. And this is the manner of the remission: every creditor shall remit the claim that is held against a neighbor, not exacting it of a neighbor who is a member of the community, because the LORD's remission has been proclaimed" (Deut 15:1-2).

Every seven years, all debts of all Israelites were to be forgiven (Deut 15:1-11). To accomplish this, of course, would require a massive redistribution of wealth. No liquid wealth was hereditary (although holding land—an Israelite's birthright—could be passed to future generations). Therefore every seven years, when all debts were forgiven, wealth was inevitably redistributed. In essence those who through misfortune or even poor management had sunk into poverty over that seven-year period would, through the forgiving of their debts, receive a transfer of wealth in order that they could begin all over again.

The sabbatical year also contained provisions regarding slavery (Deut 15:12-18). The institution of slavery was profoundly different in Israel than it was in Egypt, Assyria, Babylon, Rome—or the United States. The Israelite slave was more an indentured servant than "chattel," who agreed temporarily to service of a "master" as a way of paying off debts. Therefore Deuteronomy commands that no slave could be held beyond six years except by his or her consent. On the sabbatical year, each slave throughout Israel was to be set free. Intriguingly Deuteronomy is quite specific in stating that these regulations applied to female as well as male slaves.

The final regulation of the sabbatical year does not appear in Deuteronomy but in Exodus and later became associated with the sabbatical year: the land was to lie fallow so that it could renew itself (Ex 23:10-11). With no fertilizers except animal dung to renew the earth, it had to "rest" in order to be able to continue to provide sufficient crops for the Israelites.

A second way to redistribute income was through *loans*. Because of the sabbatical year, it is reasonable to assume that the wealthy would hesitate to provide loans to those struggling in the economy. Deuteronomy instructs them not to be hesitant. The law commands that loans are to be given between the sabbatical years. And the primary stipulation on such loans is that they are to be given without interest (Deut 23:19-20). The purpose of giving a loan was not to make money but to help your neighbor in need. So to charge interest on a loan would take advantage of the vulnerability of your neighbor, who would not have requested a loan if he or she were not already in trouble. Such loans were not only to be interest free; they were automatically to be forgiven on the sabbatical year, no matter how little had been paid back or how late in the sabbatical cycle they were granted (Deut 15:7-11). There was to be no making of money on the misfortune of other Jews.

A third way income was to be redistributed was through *the tithe*. Each Israelite was expected to give a tithe of his or her wealth annually to the king and judiciary, a second tithe to the Levites and religious leaders (because they were not permitted to hold land) and a third tithe to the poor (Deut 14:22-29; 16:1-17). One tithe was to be given at each of the three festivals every Jew was required to attend annually: the Passover, the Festival of First Fruits and the Festival of Booths. The tithe for the poor was to be given at the Festival of First Fruits (Deut 26:1-15), and how it was to be given is particularly intriguing.

"A wandering Aramean was my ancestor; he went down into Egypt and lived there as an alien" (Deut 26:5). First, the giving of 10 percent of one's annual income to the poor happens within the context of reciting one's origins as a people. Individual identity is directly linked to the community of which the individual is a part. This is profoundly relational. In essence, Deuteronomy says, "You are part of a culture—a corporate identity that existed before you were born and after you have died—that profoundly shapes you, names you, identifies you. Who you are is who your people have been and will be, and therefore you must assume responsibility for one another. You give freely and generously to the poor because you are all Hebrews!"

Second, the tithe to the poor happens within the context of worship. Worship is not only our devotion to God; it is perhaps the most profound expression of a people's cultural heritage, for their very origins as a people are caught up in their relationship with God and each other.

Third, it is done within a recital of history that requires those giving the money to remind themselves and all who listen that they were once also poor and powerless but are no longer because (and only because) of the miraculous intervention of God (Deut 26:5-10).

Fourth, the givers are required to distribute the tithe directly to the poor themselves; there is no government, social service or even religious body to assume this obligation. The person must give the money to the poor directly, with his or her own hands.

Finally, it is to be given within the context of a banquet. It is a time of joy and celebration for everyone—giver and receiver alike—but with the understanding that the poor, once they become financially solvent, are themselves to give away a tithe of their fortune to the poor.

There are many other instructions within Deuteronomy regarding the responsibility of the rich and middle class toward the poor of the land. But these are some of the most surprising and intriguing requirements. We see demonstrated, in even this brief synopsis of Deuteronomy, Israel's commitment to *compensatory economic justice,* for all the instructions are designed to bring to reality the assertion that "there will . . . be no one poor among you."

The prophets and the people. Besides developing the concept of the office of king, Deuteronomy also sets forth the office of *the prophet.* The role of the prophet vis-à-vis the systems is specific (Deut 18:18-20). The religious, political and economic systems are to be held accountable by the prophets. They are to speak truth to the highest political, religious and economic authorities, as well as to the people. And the truth they are to hold up before these systems is the Deuteronomic vision. They are to declare, "Thus says the LORD . . . " to the political system, calling king and judge to work for justice. The prophets are to declare the Word of God to the religious system and its leaders when they are beginning to serve other gods (like wealth) rather than Yahweh. They are to declare the judgment of God on the economic system and its leaders when they observe poverty beginning to occur in the land because of an inequitable sharing of wealth.

To fulfill this mission, Deuteronomy declares that the prophet is to have direct and personal entrée to the king, the high priest, the nobility and the wealthy. The prophet is not to be persecuted for his words. This is why Israel's and Judah's kings, who hated prophets like Jeremiah, Micah, Amos, Elijah, Nathan and Isaiah, allowed them access to the throne, and it is why the persecution of Jeremiah by the high priest was seen as such a profoundly evil act. If the prophet speaks the truth, the systems are to obey him and follow God's call to them. If the prophet speaks untruth, God (not the king) will deal with the prophet.

But Deuteronomy declares there is a sacred role for *the people* to play as well. The role of the people is twofold. First, the responsibility of the people is to live out God's intentions for the larger society (Deut 7:9-11). As the religious system is to be in relationship with God, so it is incumbent upon each Israelite to love and obey God. As the political system is to be just, so it is the responsibility of each Israelite to be just in all her dealings, not only with every other Israelite but also with every "stranger" or "alien" with whom she comes in contact. As the economic system is to be concerned with the redistribution of wealth, so each Israelite is to view his wealth as a gift from God that is not meant for him to hoard but to share freely with those most in need.

Second, each Israelite is to teach this way of life to her children (Deut 6:5-9) so that generation after generation of Israel can remain faithful to Yahweh and can contribute—each in his generation—to the implementation of God's intentions for the world.

THE SHALOM COMMUNITY

This magnificent book of Deuteronomy presents God's design for the way political, economic and religious systems, and their prophets and people are meant to function. But what can we call this design? The word I believe most effectively captures this comprehensive vision of the world is the Hebrew word *shalom*. And I would call the kind of society that seeks to live out God's intention a "shalom community."

Shalom is most often translated into English as "peace." But the English word *peace* doesn't begin to capture the nuances of *shalom*. *Peace* simply means there is no hostility occurring right now—no fighting, warfare or conflict. But the Hebrew word *shalom* means much more than the simple cessation of hostilities. *Shalom* is an exceedingly rich concept, a comprehensive word dealing with and covering all the relationships of daily life, expressing the ideal state of life in Israel and, indeed, the entire world. The concept of *shalom* essentially encompasses what the Israelites saw as being foundational to life: being in community with each other.

The fundamental meaning of *shalom* is captured by such English words as "totality," "wholeness," "well-being" and "harmony." It is a comprehensive word that includes in it

- bodily health (see, for example, Ps 38:3)
- security and strength (Judg 6:23; Dan 10:19)
- a long life ending in a natural death (Gen 15:15)

- prosperity and abundance (Job 5:18-26; Ps 37:11; Lam 3:16-17; Zech 8:12)

- successful completion of an enterprise (Judg 18:5; 1 Sam 1:17)

- victory in war (Judg 8:4-9). (Note that *shalom* does not necessarily mean a cessation of conflict; it means victory for Israel's troops.)

So when Jews wish each other "shalom," they are wishing for each other health, security, long life, prosperity, successful completion of an enterprise, victory in war. In other words, they are wishing God's best for the entirety of a person's life, for all her relationships with others, for all he sets his hand to do. And they are wishing for such fullness both for that person's life and for the Jewish community throughout the world.

It is important to recognize that *shalom* is a corporate word. It describes a community, not simply the interior well-being of an individual or a small group of people. *Shalom* captures the well-being of an entire society. Therefore it describes the political, economic and religious well-being of a people *and their systems* who are building their society upon a religion of personal and corporate relationship with God and each other, a politics of justice and an economics of equitable distribution of wealth designed to eliminate poverty within their midst. *Shalom* is therefore a political word, an economic word and a religious word that is meant to be corporate and society-wide as well as personal, individual and family-wide. There is simply no word richer or more meaningful than *shalom*.

The full nuance of the word *shalom* was carried over into Christianity by its founding Jewish Christians. Although the New Testament is written in Greek and therefore uses the Greek word *eirēnē*, the writers of these Christian Scriptures redefine *eirēnē*, rejecting its classical Greek meaning in order to fill it with all the Jews meant when they wished each other shalom.

As we will discover in chapter three, Jesus built his theology around the concept of the kingdom of God. It takes very little reading of the Gospel accounts, however, to recognize that what Jesus meant by the kingdom of God was simply the full living-out of shalom upon the earth, in its private and public dimensions, in its personal and corporate dimensions, and in its political, economic and religious systemic dimensions. The "kingdom of God" was shalom personified and particularized in the life of God's people.

The supreme gift of Jesus to his followers was to be shalom, which was to be lifted above the commonplace and the everyday to its highest level: living in unbroken union with God in the midst of the adversities of life and manifested in our union as brothers and sisters in Christ (Jn 14:27). This comes about as the result of each of us—and all of us together—embracing the life, death and resurrection of Jesus as our own and in our stead (Acts 10:36; Eph 2:17; 6:15). Full shalom, therefore, is not something we can manufacture or earn, but comes as God's free gift of *amazing* grace (Rom 1:7; 1 Cor 1:3; 2 Cor 1:2; Gal 1:3; Phil 1:2; Col 1:2; 2 Thess 1:2).

Finally, shalom is the identifying mark of the authentic church. Christ has broken down the wall of estrangement between all human dichotomies that separate and alienate us from each other (male versus female, slave versus free, parent versus child, race versus race, systems versus the people). Instead, God's free gift of shalom, continually provided for us, draws us into one body (Eph 2:14-17; Heb 7:2). This is God's continuing act of redemption, its intended scope being the restoration of the whole creation to its proper harmony (Col 1:19-22).

Consequently all of God's people are called to the universal ministry of shalom-making (Mt 5:9). We are at all times to be about the task of planting the seeds from which God can genuinely nurture shalom into full fruit in the life of the whole world (Rom 14:19; 15:33; 16:20; 1 Cor 14:33; 2 Cor 13:11; Eph 4:3; Phil 4:7; 2 Thess 3:16; Heb 12:11; 13:20; Jas 3:16-18).[5]

The Hebrew concept of shalom and its Christian development is a rich one that best captures the vision for human society presented in Deuteronomy. The message of Deuteronomy is that the shalom community is an achievable society of political justice and economic equity birthed in and resulting in a relational culture. That society comes about in all its power when such a culture is centered in that nation's love for God. This is how to know God—not to engage in privatized acts of piety but to "do justice and to love each other tenderly and to walk humbly with your God" (Mic 6:8, author's adaptation). This is God's design for your neighborhood, your school, your business, your city, your nation—and for you!

The dream of the shalom community is a golden thread woven through the entirety of Scripture. Various biblical writers and leaders call it by different names: the peaceable kingdom, a new heaven and a new earth, the kingdom of God, the New Jerusalem. But in each of these, the same essential vision is being presented of a life together in a God-based society. (To sample that vision moving through the Bible, reflect on the Scriptures listed in the following endnote.[6])

For more than thirty-five hundred years, the vision of shalom community has presented for God's people a paradigm of what human life should be about. And it has been successfully practiced and continues to be practiced in societies, in cities and in nations around the world. One such practice of the shalom community has been going on for almost fifteen hundred years—and continues today. That is the Benedictine monastic movement.

Benedict of Nursia (circa 480-543) was a young nobleman in the Roman Empire who quickly grew weary of its vices and frivolity. He therefore entered into the monastic life but found life from one monastery to another unpredictable and quixotic. Benedict envisioned a corporate monastic existence in which authority would be centered in an abbot but all monks would share in deliberation, wealth would be perceived as common rather than private and would be equitably shared, and monastic life would be centered in the worship of God. Around 529, Benedict founded his own monastery, Monte Cassino, about halfway between Naples and Rome. (Intriguingly, Monte Cassino continued as an active monastery until World War II, when it was destroyed in a bombing attack.)

To govern the monastery, Benedict wrote what would become his famed *Rule of St. Benedict,* a carefully designed compendium of instructions that guaranteed that all Benedictine monasteries would be operated justly, in an equitable economic manner, and centered in the worship of God. The compendium set a standard for monastic life that swept across Europe, transforming the monastic movement, providing an alternative economy and distribution of power to that of lords and serfs, and spearheading the evangelistic and social conversion of Europe to the Christian God.[7]

One of my spiritual disciplines is to go periodically on silent retreat at St. Andrew's Abbey, a Benedictine monastery in the high desert of Southern California. Warmly welcomed each time by the monks following the fifteen-hundred-year *Rule* regarding hospitality, I join with the brothers, priests and fellow retreatants in the five periods of daily worship, the singing of the Psalms, the corporate meals—often accompanied by silence or by listening to a book read aloud—and observing the monks at work as I take walks of reflection. While the monastery is built around worship and work, I am impressed by the unique combination of peace and joy that fills the place as the brothers live, work, share resources, care for one another and praise God together.

What is most unique about St. Andrew's, however, is that those who founded this monastery were a group of Belgian Benedictines who had been missionaries to China for more than thirty years before being driven out by the Maoist revolution. And now they are on a mission to Southern California, teaching in the universities, practicing medicine, caring for the poor and providing hospitality and retreat. Yes, the shalom community is alive and well both in the high desert of Southern California and through the Benedictines around the world.

The shalom community is the biblical vision of the world as God intended it to be—society as it should be. It should therefore give God's people direction, mission and focus for our work and witness in the world. It is this vision that we—the church—should be about. In the final analysis, we are not called to build bigger or better churches, to prepare disciples or even to win people to Jesus Christ, though these are all important and strategic elements. We as the church are to focus on working for the realization of the shalom community in our political, economic and religious life together. *That* mission of proclaiming the vision and doing whatever we can to move this world toward "becoming the kingdom of our Lord and of His Christ" is the essence of what we Christians are to be about.

2

WHAT KEEPS
GOING WRONG?

Evil That Is More Than Personal

IN THE PREVIOUS CHAPTER WE EXAMINED the biblical vision of human society as God meant it to be. But that biblical vision is certainly not descriptive of our cities or nations as we experience them today. Therefore the questions we must ask are, Why is there such disparity? Is the vision unrealistic, unachievable? Or is there something within us and our systems that keeps on making our lives and our cities such a mess? What went wrong? And what keeps going wrong?

The Bible not only presents a clear vision of human society as God intended it to be; it also presents an analysis of the nature and results of corporate sin. The Scripture is full of a surprisingly consistent social analysis of how and why the world's political, economic and religious systems have become so corrupt. And that biblical analysis makes clear that evil is not only personal but also profoundly social.

Perhaps the clearest analysis of the sinfulness of human society is found in the book of Ezekiel. From its first to its forty-eighth chapter, Ezekiel examines what went wrong with Israelite society and what God is doing and will do to correct that wrong. But one of Ezekiel's most pithy analyses of the evil bent of human society is found in Ezekiel 22.

The Bloody City

> The word of the LORD came to me: You, mortal, will you judge, will you judge the bloody city? Then declare to it all its abominable deeds. You shall say, Thus says the Lord GOD: A city! Shedding blood within itself; its time has come; making its idols, defiling itself. You have become guilty by the blood that you have shed, and defiled by the idols that you have made; you have brought your day near, the appointed time of your years has come. Therefore I have made you a disgrace before the nations, and a mockery to all the countries. (Ezek 22:1-4)

This prophecy was written just before the final conquest of Judah (or the Southern Kingdom)—all that was left of Israel[1]—by the Babylonian empire. In this chapter, Jerusalem is a symbol for Israel as it faces its final destruction.

The message of Ezekiel in chapter 22 is very painful. Jerusalem will be conquered by Babylon, and in its destruction all that is left of Israel will be eliminated. Israel will be no more, and the dream of God's shalom community will seem extinguished from the earth. What has brought God's people to such a tragic place?

Ezekiel 22 can be divided into three parts. Part one consists of verses 1 through 12. In this section, Ezekiel explains why God is so angry. Israel has abandoned God's call to be a nation of shalom in both its actions and its rhetoric. Instead it has become so immoral that it has become a reverse witness to God; the rest of the world looks at the lifestyle of Israel and concludes, "If that is what it is like to follow Yahweh, then let me follow a far more just god like Baal." Thus God's people, who were chosen to introduce the shalom community to the world, have become the worse kind of evangelist, for they witness to every other nation against Yahweh rather than for God and God's kingdom.

Part two consists of verses 13 through 22. It takes the argument a step further by presenting what God is going to do with Israel in light of their extreme unfaithfulness. God will destroy Israel in order to purge the evil from it, for it can no longer be trusted to carry the vision of the shalom community. After its captivity by Babylonia, a remnant of Israel will emerge—those who have personally embraced relationship with God and justice and equality with humanity—and that remnant will create a future for Israel.

But it is part three that contains one of the clearest and most significant social analyses in Scripture. Whereas part one asks, "What went wrong?"

42

and part two asks, "What will be the result of such wrongdoing?" part three asks, "What were the forces that caused Israel to go astray? How did they wander so far from God's intentions for them?"

A RELIGION OF DOMINATION

> Its priests have done violence to my teaching and have profaned my holy things; they have made no distinction between the holy and the common, neither have they taught the difference between the unclean and the clean, and they have disregarded my sabbaths, so that I am profaned among them. (Ezek 22:26)

To make sense of Ezekiel's critique of the religious community, one must ask, "How did Israelites at the time of Ezekiel believe they could come into a right relationship with God?" The answer is, through obedience to the law of Moses. But how were Israelites to know what the law required of them, since most could not read? They could only know if the priests told them.

That is the point of Ezekiel's analysis of Judah's religious system: "[The religious system has] made no distinction between the holy and the common, neither have they taught the difference between the unclean and the clean, and they have disregarded my sabbaths" (Ezek 22:26). God entrusted into the hands of the priests the responsibility of sharing the information the people needed in order to obey the law and act rightly before God. But the priests refused to give the people the information they needed so that they might act obediently toward the law. The priests didn't tell the people whether what they were doing was clean or unclean, holy or common, sacred or secular.

Why would religious leaders refuse to give people the information they need in order to be in a right relationship with God? The withholding of vital information places control in the hands of the priests. If I don't give you the information you need and you become increasingly desperate for that information, I am able to control you as long as I withhold that information. And if I am able to control you over a long period, I can begin to dominate you in every way.

Of course this is the essential weakness of any system that helps to set and maintain the values and beliefs of a society. That system can move very easily from believing in its values to using its growing authority to press these values on the people "for their own good." When it does so, the values it promulgates will subtly shift so that the system will seek to build its power through insisting upon its values and will twist those values so they serve the purposes of the political and economic powers of its society. This is what the professional religionists of Ezekiel's world were doing: they were creating a *religion of domination.*

Thus any of the values-forming systems of any nation—not simply the church and religion but also the public and private educational systems, the world of entertainment, the media, communications and information-provision systems (newspapers, television news, radio, Internet and so on), the world of advertising, the business world, the sports world—can use their power to provide information to control the thinking of entire generations of that nation and even of the world. And once their ideas become successful in controlling the thinking of people, then these systems can create a culture of dominance in which they shape the way an entire people think and what they value. Thus a culture of dominance can emerge and replace a relational culture.

Recently I was invited to lecture on the systems in the business department of a Christian college. During the course of my lecture, I asked the students what should be the chief objective of a business run by Christians. "To make a profit," one student answered. I asked the class if they agreed or disagreed. Everyone agreed. So I countered that, to my mind, Christians have the obligation to run their businesses with the primary objective of producing high-quality goods or providing the best service, and the *result* of such quality work would be both a high volume of business resulting in a profit and a witness to their faith that relationships are more important than money. They thought that was hopelessly naive. One student put it most succinctly: "I have no problem in producing a product I know is inferior or to provide poor service, because I want to keep my costs down. That's okay because what I care about is making as much money as possible." Thus had these "Christian" students adopted the values of their culture and of its economic and political systems that would lead them to run their businesses with premises no different from those who might run an Enron or WorldCom.

A POLITICS OF OPPRESSION

[Israel's] princes within it are like a roaring lion tearing the prey; they have devoured human lives; they have taken treasure and precious things; they have made many widows within it. (Ezek 22:25)

The next system with which Ezekiel dealt was the political system. Its task, according to the Deuteronomic vision, is to work through judicial and monarchial structures for justice for all the people. But what have the "princes" done with this responsibility? Ezekiel informs us they have "devoured human lives; they have taken treasure and precious things; they have made many widows within it." Most intriguingly, they are likened to "a roaring lion tearing the prey."

Those entrusted with the responsibility of equitably administering justice have instead become those who are oppressors of the people. Their concern has shifted from upholding justice to wielding power. The reference to "made many widows" is a reference to the Josian wars in which King Josiah took advantage of the collapse of the Assyrian empire to expand Israel's landmass, conquer nations and restore the empire boundaries of Israel's greatest king, David. The price paid was the death of an entire generation of young men in a fruitless war (thus Ezekiel's reference to the princes making many widows in the nation), and such a serious weakening of the nation's military strength that Babylonia, once recuperated from its defeat of Assyria, could easily conquer Israel's army, take Jerusalem and destroy Judah within twenty-three years.

Ezekiel's analysis of what went wrong politically in Israel was that the political system called by God to order society through justice for all had instead become an oppressor of the most vulnerable people and groups of that society. Rather than guaranteeing justice, the political system had practiced a *politics of oppression*. This is precisely the great temptation of every political system since time immemorial—to serve its own ends and to join with economic and religious systems to accrue power at the expense of the people, even if that means the oppression and control of that people.

AN ECONOMICS OF EXPLOITATION

Its officials within it are like wolves tearing the prey, shedding blood, destroying lives to get dishonest gain. . . . They take bribes to shed blood;

[they] take both advance interest and accrued interest, and make gain of [their] neighbors by extortion; and [they] have forgotten me, says the Lord GOD. (Ezek 22:27, 12)

The word *officials* is a reference to the economic system of the nation. The responsibility of the economic system, according to Deuteronomy, is to be faithful stewards of the nation's wealth so there can be an equitable distribution of that wealth in order to eliminate poverty. But what did Israel's economic leaders do?

The business leaders of Israel had moved from seeing the purpose of business as providing a service or quality goods, to seeing it as making the biggest profit possible. They took bribes. They charged interest in their loans—something explicitly forbidden in the law. They extorted. They had brought about a profound change in what they perceived as the mission of business.

What had occurred in Israel was a significant shift in the thinking and actions of its economic leaders. They had moved from seeing the wealth of Israel as God's wealth held in common for the entire society to perceiving themselves as the principal owners of private wealth. Thus they had changed from understanding themselves as *stewards* to viewing themselves as *owners*. The result of that shift was a profound change in the way Israel's economic leaders used the nation's wealth, for they used it for their own purposes and profit, intentionally exploiting the poor, marginalized and powerless of that society to increase their wealth. They were practicing an *economics of exploitation*.

It is fitting here to note that Ezekiel uses the phrase "wolves tearing their prey" to describe the economic system, whereas he uses the term "roaring lion" to describe the political system (Ezek 22:25). It is worth speculating on what Ezekiel had in mind by likening these two systems to these two specific animals. I believe that the key to understanding these mysterious references is to consider the hunting styles of both creatures.

The lion stalks its intended prey, seeking to get into striking distance without being seen. It does this because it does not possess great speed and must therefore use the element of surprise to catch its prey. Having come within striking distance, it springs from the cover, then pursues and captures its intended prey. It strikes by leaping on the animal's back, bringing its three hundred to five hundred pounds down on an animal that might weigh between fifty and three hundred pounds. As the animal falls, the lion uses its powerful jaws to sever either the spinal cord or the jugular vein. The kill is quick, clean and complete in one swift action.

The wolf hunts in an entirely different manner. Although it will eat rabbits and rodents as a dietary mainstay, the wolf's favorite meal is elk, moose or deer. Not possessing the strength or weight of a lion, a wolf must hunt in a pack to bring down prey weighing between five hundred and eight hundred pounds. The strategy the wolf pack uses to accomplish this objective is to get a herd running. Possessing the endurance to run at high speed for long periods of time, the wolf pack begins to wear out the herd. Gradually the youngest, oldest and weakest fall to the rear. The pack selects one of the most vulnerable, culls it from the rest of the herd and proceeds to bring it down. This they do by stopping the animal and then tearing its Achilles tendons. The paralyzed animal sinks to the ground. The wolf pack does not usually kill the animal; they simply gather around it and begin eating it. Weakened by loss of blood, flesh and muscle, and in great pain, the animal dies.

By likening the lion to the political system and the wolf to the economic system, Ezekiel is making a profound analogy about the capacity of both systems to dominate and control their societies. The political system is a discernibly dominating power. It "kills" its intended victims directly and efficiently, using the law, police or military as its instrument of elimination. It understands and uses both violence and the threat of violence as its primary means of domination, and it does so under the the laws it has created both to protect itself and to dominate and control its "subjects" (even its language is dominating).

The economic system, which is not given the powers of the law, police or military, must "kill" in a different way. It cannot appear overtly violent. Instead it must gain economic dominance over the people by setting the economic, and sometimes the social, standards of a society ("herding" the people), pressuring the society to vigorously pursue those standards ("running the herd") and then noting those who do not have the economic power, education, capacity or position to stay up with the rest of the herd. The economic system thus "culls" the weakest, most marginalized and most vulnerable people and people groups that will become its intended victims. Those groups that will tend to be most vulnerable are the poorest and least powerful groups: dominated ethnic groups, women, those without invested wealth and those whose social standards differ from the norm. Because these "minorities" are perceived as "different" and even unacceptable by the general public, their exploitation will tend to receive the least notice or defense by that public (running elk don't return to protect the weak who have been culled by the wolf pack).

The economic system doesn't destroy its victims quickly; to do so would lessen that system's capacity to make money off them. Instead they "nip" and "bite" at their "prey," little by little weakening them rather than quickly killing them, so that the economic system "eats alive" the economically weakest and most marginalized segments of that society. And the rest of that society never even notices what is happening.

The credit card is a simple example of this. It is an efficient means by which a user borrows money from a bank or financial institution to make purchases. In reality, the credit card's purpose is to increase debt while encouraging a growing economy by increasing the spending capacity of the people. The "religious," values-creating systems of advertising, the media, entertainment and sports encourage the purchase of goods as the primary means by which we can both improve our lifestyle and bring fulfillment or joy to life. The political system cooperates by making an exception to the nation's laws of usury so that credit card providers can charge compound interest on unpaid credit card debts that exceed what the law allows financial institutions to charge for any other medium of loan.

Thus every system "wins." The retail business community makes a greater profit by radically increasing sales. The production community makes a profit through increased production of goods. The financial community makes excessive profit by charging compound interest on unpaid credit card debts. The political system radically increases its tax base on the goods sold. The values-formation communities (advertising, communications, sports and so on) make residual profits through the generation of more advertising, sports endorsements, and so on.

And who loses? The poor and the marginalized. They are as encouraged to "shop till you drop" as are the rich and middle class. But it is the poor and marginalized who have the most to lose in participating in this vehicle of purchase. The rich and some in the middle class can afford and choose to pay off all their purchases each month, thus avoiding high interest rates. But the poor and many overextended middle-class people cannot afford such monthly payoffs and soon find themselves both in inextricable debt and owing exorbitant interest.

But the victims of the credit card phenomenon are not just the poor and marginalized. The seducing call of our economic, political and religious systems (especially the advertising industry) to purchase more has resulted in an accumulation of credit card debt that moves far beyond the poor and working classes to most of the middle class and even among the well-to-do. Thus credit card debt has grown from 56 percent of disposable income in 1983 to 81 percent by 1995. Twenty-nine thousand personal bankruptcies now occur *every week* in the United States. One third of all Americans have no savings. Another third have less than three thousand dollars in investments and savings. And while people wallow in such shocking debt, our national government tells us that the patriotic way to respond to terrorist attacks is to spend and spend and spend some more.[2]

By likening the political system to lions and the economic system to wolves, Ezekiel has made a profound commentary on how each of these systems pursues domination of its society. With his insightful analysis of the priestly strategies used to gain control over the shaping of the values of a society, Ezekiel has shown how systems act to dominate rather than to liberate.

A DANGEROUSLY DESCENDING SPIRAL

Whereas one can describe a godly society in terms of an *ascending spiral* of humanity coming into an ever-expanding relationship with God, an increasingly just political system and an equitable economic system that eliminates poverty, here Ezekiel is clearly describing the exact opposite. Presenting that dynamic as a *descending spiral,* he perceives that the decay of a society begins with its economic system, when managers make as great a profit for themselves as possible, no matter how much that leads to the exploitation of the people. The more the economic system exploits the people, the more it needs to call upon the political system to use power to oppress by creating and interpreting laws to favor the economic system. Thus the collusion of the political system with the economic system allows for and permits greater exploitation.

But a political system can oppress only so far before it begins to lose its credibility with the people. Thus it must depend on those structures in society that create, teach and maintain that society's values to "bless" the political and economic systems. In our society those structures include public and private education at all levels, marketing, entertainment, news media, and even professional sports. Thus the "religious" system uses its influence of persuasion, emotion and logic to maintain the people's obedience to and support of these systems. Such control of people's priorities, values and beliefs then gives permission to the economic system to undertake even greater exploitation, which it inevitably will do.

How do we see this spiral of domination at work in society? How do we see systems in collusion together to use their respective powers to oppress, exploit and control the responses of the people? Consider the accumulation of wealth and power in the hands of a very few, which is happening very rapidly in the United States.

Between 1979 and 1995, male college graduates realized an increase of only 1 percent in their income (averaging for cost of living). High school graduates experienced a decline of 17 percent in the buying power of their income. And those who did not graduate from high school had a 27 percent decrease.[3] Meanwhile the CEOs of the one hundred largest companies in the United States each went from an average annual income of 1.3 million dollars to 37.5 million dollars—one thousand times the pay of their production crews! According to a 2002 New York Times Magazine article, "The 13,000 richest families in America had almost as much income [in 1998] as the 20 million poorest households."[4] However, the richest gave 35 percent of all campaign dollars in recent presidential elections. Guess who gets more of a hearing?[5]

The more the economic system exploits, the more the political system will oppress. The more oppression occurs, the more the values-creating system must control and shape people's thinking. Control leads to greater exploitation that leads to greater oppression that leads to greater control that leads to greater exploitation, and on and on and on and on. This continues until the society has so decayed that it is fast approaching its own internal collapse or external destruction.

THE PROPHETS SEDUCED

What can stop the declining spiral of the economic, political and "religious" systems of a city or nation? According to Deuteronomy, the reformist forces in society are the prophets and the people. But note what Ezekiel states happens to the prophets and people in a society in which the systems are growing increasingly corrupt: "Its prophets have smeared whitewash on their behalf, seeing false visions and divining lies for them, saying, 'Thus says the Lord GOD,' when the LORD has not spoken" (Ezek 22:28).

The prophets were to be the voice of God, holding the systems of society accountable for fulfilling the specific roles God had created for them. But what have the prophets of Judah done with their responsibility to call their king, priests and merchants to accountability? They have "smeared whitewash" over all the misdeeds of these systems, covering with a coat of white paint the acts of exploitation, oppression and control of Israel's systems as they sought to dominate both God and the people of Israel.

Worse yet, the prophets have also attempted to fool the people and the systems into thinking that they were doing the will of God by operating dominating systems. Ezekiel is making an extremely severe criticism here, since Deuteronomy had declared, "But any prophet who . . . presumes to speak in my name a word that I have not commanded the prophet to speak—that prophet shall die" (Deut 18:20). Thus, by lying, the prophets of Israel were either defying God or indicating that they really didn't believe in Yahweh after all.

Consider the prophet Hananiah (Jer 28:1-17). Hananiah was the preferred prophet in Israel who prophesied that God would soon destroy Babylon and return its Jewish captives to Judah. Jeremiah took him to task, declaring that his prophecy was wrong and, in fact, a deceit (v. 1). Hananiah refused to accept Jeremiah's rebuke and used his power and influence to undermine Jeremiah's credibility. Jeremiah responded, "Listen, Hananiah, the LORD has not sent you, and you made this people trust in a lie. Therefore thus says the LORD: I am going to send you off the face of the earth. Within this year you will be dead, because you have spoken rebellion against the LORD." That is exactly what happened (Jer 28:15-17)!

Why would a prophet lie, knowing the extreme consequences of a lie? A key is given in the words "Hananiah . . . spoke to me in the house of the LORD, in the presence of the priests and all the people" (Jer 28:1). Hananiah was benefitting greatly from giving a false prophecy. He was receiving the attention, trust and adulation of the people and was probably receiving great benefit from the king, the priests and the business establishment for strengthening their domination of the people rather than questioning it.

The systems do not want to be held accountable. They cannot freely dominate the people and at the same time be accountable to the heavenly vision for the city or nation. Therefore leaders of the political, economic and religious systems will do whatever they can to seduce the prophet—to buy him off with praise, attention, prestige, money or position. And if they fail to seduce him, the systems will find ways to "kill" him, either physically or in reputation.

In the United States today, I would not count the church among the "religious" systems. Christianity has become too marginalized to be a significant values-creating system for any but its own constituency. That is why I believe a significant role to which the church in the United States is being called is that of prophet. It needs to be a voice crying, "Thus saith the LORD," to the political, economic and values-creating systems of our society. The church must stand before the systems and pressure them to be just, equitable and relational in all they do.

But to the degree that the church is successful in that pursuit, to that same degree the systems will seek to seduce or threaten the church. So beware when the city council wants to give your church a plaque or invites you to open their sessions with prayer or suggests a program your church can perform for the poor and offers you the funding to carry that out. Beware if it uses zoning rules to stop you from building a church or threatens a lawsuit or engages in character assassination. The systems will do everything they can to seduce or "kill" church leaders who threaten their capacity to dominate, control, oppress or exploit.

THE PEOPLE CO-OPTED

> The people of the land have practiced extortion and committed robbery; they have oppressed the poor and needy, and have extorted from the alien without redress. And I sought for anyone among them who would repair the wall and stand in the breach before me on behalf of the land, so that I would not destroy it; but I found no one. (Ezek 22:29-30)

The second reformist force is the people. In the Deuteronomic formula, the task of the people is to apply to their own lives God's call to the systems, to teach this way of life to their children and, in so doing, to hold the systems accountable to act out their responsibilities. But Ezekiel presents one of the saddest results of systems that have become dominating, oppressive and exploitive: the darkest characteristics of the systems are passed on to the people.

Seeing the systems "grabbing for all they can get," the people begin imitating the systems. Even though those values of greed, power and domination are unarticulated, the people hear those values expressed in the actions of the systems. And the people consequently begin to embrace those values as their own. Toward each other, and especially toward the most vulnerable in their midst, the people also become dominating, oppressive and exploitive. So it is that God seeks "for anyone among them who would . . . stand in the breach before me on behalf of the [people], so that I would not destroy it; *but I found no one!*" (Ezek 22:30, emphasis mine).

Is this not what is happening to our culture today? A recent advertisement on radio and television depicts a small town where the streets are empty, the porches deserted, the people no longer gather to visit with each other. "Where are all the people?" the advertisement asks. Then we discover them. They are at home, all of them accessing the Internet in order to trade on the stock market and to make a great deal of money. "Where did old Mr. Jones get the money for such a fancy red convertible?" the advertisement ends. And it informs us that he got the money from successfully playing the stock market on the Internet.

Isn't it tragic that the advertisement promoting such a use of the Internet presents this message of empty streets and the destruction of the relational culture of that town *as a positive change?* Its premise is that the chief end of human beings is to make as much money as possible. It doesn't reveal that what it is proposing will destroy us, if truly embraced by the people, for we will surrender the common good.

Ezekiel 22 teaches that when systems become corrupt enough they will relentlessly corrupt the prophets and the people who will be seduced by them and will join with them in their exploitation, oppression and control of that society. The people will be infected with the systems' greed. Thus the only forces that can work to hold the systems accountable will themselves become a part of the corruption of that society. And when that happens and keeps on happening, there is no hope for that nation or civilization.

THE INEVITABLE END

> Therefore I have poured out my indignation upon them; I have consumed them with the fire of my wrath; I have returned their conduct upon their heads, says the Lord GOD. (Ezek 22:31)

Within these final words in the prophecy of The Bloody City, the greatest tragedy lies. When society has sunk far enough, Ezekiel tells us, God has no choice but to destroy it. That is precisely what happened to Israel. The people who were to witness to the rest of the world how God intended all humanity to live would become the people who had embraced the priorities of personal wealth, oppression and exploitation that symbolized the worship of the god Baal. This is how the nation called out of slavery by God would end: political, economic and religious systems corrupted beyond their capacity to be reformed, religious leaders seduced by the power and wealth of the systems, and a people who were aping their leaders in an equal pursuit for control, power and money. Such a society, Ezekiel tells us, will inevitably collapse and end.

And how will it end? Here come the most depressing words of Ezekiel. God says to Ezekiel, "I have poured out my indignation upon them. . . . *I have returned their conduct upon their heads,* says the Lord GOD" (Ezek 22:31, emphasis mine). God will bring about the collapse of that nation *by doing nothing!* God will simply let that nation's inevitable collapse happen. No great defeat at the hands of an enemy is needed. God will lift a hand of blessing off that nation and simply let it experience the consequences of its own actions. God will allow the systems, out of their greed and commitment to domination, to destroy themselves. The nation and its people will collapse. God will let them "reap the whirlwind" from the wind they have sown (Hos 8:7).

Ezekiel presents this collapse in the most graphic terms. Before the Babylonian captivity, there was a mysterious glow over the temple (and over the tabernacle before the temple was built). This phenomenon was reported in Exodus 40:34-35; Leviticus 16:2; Numbers 9:15; 1 Kings 8:10; 2 Chronicles 5:13 and 7:2; Isaiah 6:4; and Haggai 2:7-9 as well as by Ezekiel. The Hebrew Bible makes it very clear that this glow or "luminous cloud" was the manifestation that Yahweh was present in the temple and among the Hebrew people. This glow was called the *shekinah.*

In Ezekiel 10—11, the following event was recorded:

Now the cherubim [angelic creatures] were standing on the south side of the [temple] when the man went in; and a cloud filled the inner court. Then the glory of the LORD rose up from the cherub to the threshold of the house; the house was filled with the cloud, and the court was full of the brightness of the glory of the LORD. . . . *Then the glory of the LORD went out from the threshold of the house and stopped above the cherubim.* The cherubim lifted up their wings and rose up from the earth in my sight as they went out. . . . They stopped at the entrance of the east gate of the house of the LORD; and the glory of the God of Israel was above them. . . . *And the glory of the LORD ascended from the middle of the city, and stopped on the mountain east of the city.* (Ezek 10:3-4, 18-19; 11:23; emphasis mine)

This is a terrifying commentary by Ezekiel. He tells us in this passage that the glory of God—the *shekinah*—has departed from the temple, from Jerusalem and from Israel. It went to "the mountain east of the city," where it settled down and waited for Israel to collapse. God had lifted the protective presence from Israel, and the nation and its people were now on their own. The inevitable result would be Israel's destruction.[6]

Ezekiel 22 presents us with one biblical analysis of what went wrong and what keeps going wrong in society, so that the systems act to exploit rather than to empower the people. However, many other instances in Scripture undertake the same social analysis. See also Exodus 1:8; 5:2; 1 Kings 5:13-17; 9:15-21; 10:14-27; 18:20-40; 21:1-24; 22:1-40; Matthew 23:1-39; Acts 22:30—23:35; Ephesians 2:11-22; 3:7-13; and Revelation 17—18.

This social analysis throughout Scripture tells us that whatever your class, race or background, you are radically influenced by the values and practices of the economic, political and religious systems of your country and of the world. And when those systems increasingly embrace an economics of greed and exploitation, a politics of dominating power and oppression and a "religion" of values-maintaining control, then you are on your way to becoming a person who will internally embrace those same values and will thus become increasingly centered on accumulation, control and greed, more captured by your culture than by your faith, less concerned for the poor and marginalized among you, and less able to cry for your nation's embrace of the shalom community.

POSTSCRIPT

This is not zero-sum economics. I can't find in Scripture any suggestion that wealth is fixed. The biblical economy was a growing economy, though not the aggressive growth economy we know today. What the biblical writers were insisting is that a nation's economy must be socially responsible. When speaking of a nation's economy, I use the word *equitable* rather than *equal*. *Equal* would mean an identical distribution of wealth, operating out of the perspective that there is only a static amount of wealth to be distributed. *Equitable,* on the other hand, suggests carefully constructed vehicles in an economy to periodically redistribute wealth so that no one in that economy experiences either extreme poverty or extreme wealth. The biblical point is simply this: There is no excuse for poverty existing in a world of abundance.

Second, some have suggested that the Deuteronomic vision of the equitable distribution of wealth and the elimination of poverty is the advocacy of communism and the Ezekiel critique an attack against capitalism. Such an argument is a misunderstanding of both capitalism and communism, and the Israelite economy before the Babylonian captivity. Communist economics is state ownership of the means of production, and a market economy centers its means of production in the private sector. Neither was true of pre-exilic Israel. Biblical economics was birthed in an agrarian society with shared production on birthright land. As Israel became more "settled," it increasingly embraced an economy like the surrounding nations, with land and the means of production centered in a political and economic elite living off the surplus of its peasants. The Deuteronomic and jubilee legislation of Leviticus were attempts to return the country to the economic principles on which it was founded.

The systems of every city, nation, business or church engage in continual struggle between the system's highest calling and its most destructive tendencies. How we as God's people are to join in that struggle by working for the shalom of our city, nation or world is what we will explore in the ensuing chapters. And we will begin by looking at the life, words and actions of the one who most captures our praise, adoration and imitation—Jesus Christ our Lord!

3

WHAT WAS JESUS ABOUT?

FOR CHRISTIANS TO FORMULATE a biblical theology of power that can transform our community, we must begin with the one who is the Lord of our church—Jesus Christ. What was the mission of the One we call Lord and Savior, and how did he act out that mission? What were his beliefs about power? And what insights from Jesus' mission can inform the mission we are called to undertake in God's world gone awry? Let's look at one such answer to these questions—the answer given by the Gospel writer Luke.

LUKE'S JUBILEE JESUS

> When [Jesus] came to Nazareth, where he had been brought up, he went to the synagogue on the sabbath day, as was his custom. He stood up to read, and the scroll of the prophet Isaiah was given to him. He unrolled the scroll and found the place where it was written: "The Spirit of the Lord is upon me, because he has anointed me to bring good news to the poor. He has sent me to proclaim release to the captives and recovery of sight to the blind, to let the oppressed go free, to proclaim the year of the Lord's favor." And he rolled up the scroll, gave it back to the attendant, and sat down. . . . Then he began to say to them, "Today this Scripture has been fulfilled in your hearing." (Lk 4:16-21)

Luke 4:16-21 is the pivotal passage of the Gospel of Luke. It is the mission statement of Jesus. The remainder of Luke is the acting out of the Scripture Jesus read in the synagogue that sabbath day. This passage is the key to understanding the agenda of Jesus.

Luke's story of Jesus' reading of this passage from Isaiah reveals an amazingly disparate response by the people. Luke tells us, "All spoke well of him and were amazed at the gracious words that came from his mouth" (Lk 4:22). But he also tells us that, upon Jesus' subsequent remarks, "all in the synagogue were filled with rage" to such an extent that some of them tried to kill him (Lk 4:28-29). What would have elicited such extreme and opposite reactions?

In this, Jesus' inaugural sermon, the young rabbi uses Scripture to describe what his ministry is going to be. Jesus tells his listeners he has come to

• proclaim good news to the poor

• set captives free

• recover the sight of the blind

• set at liberty those who are oppressed

• proclaim "the year of the Lord's favor"

What does Jesus mean by this description of his ministry? And why do some of the people hear him with great joy while others are enraged enough by his words to attempt to take his life?

The Scripture from which Jesus read is Isaiah 61:1-2. But there are significant differences between the Isaiah passage and the passage Jesus actually read. They agree on the calling ("anointed") and the filling by the "Spirit of the Lord" of God's servant. They agree that he has come to bring good news to the poor, to proclaim liberty to the prisoners and "to proclaim the year of the Lord's favor." But Isaiah 61 doesn't include a key phrase that Jesus spoke: "to let the oppressed go free," which is actually found in Isaiah 58:6.

But the most important difference between Isaiah 61 and Luke 4 is that whereas Jesus ends his quotation of Isaiah with the words "to proclaim the year of the Lord's favor," Isaiah continues the sentence to include the words "and the day of vengeance of our God" (Is 61:2). In other words, *Jesus stopped his reading midsentence.* That, in turn, places the emphasis not on the judgment that God will visit upon God's people, but on the proclamation of "the year of the Lord's favor." *That* was what Jesus wished to leave the listener focused on.

What is "the year of the Lord's favor" that Jesus wants so strongly to proclaim? And why does the proclamation of that year result in captives being freed, rights being restored to the oppressed and empowering news being shared with all who are poor? "The year of the Lord's favor" was a biblical way of referring to the jubilee. Both Isaiah 61 and 58 are universally recognized as passages about the Year of Jubilee. Both "to proclaim the year of the Lord's favor" and "to let the oppressed go free" were jubilee expressions. Jesus was proclaiming to Israel a Year of Jubilee!

The word *jubilee* literally means in Hebrew "the blowing of the Ram's Horn." It was a celebration based upon the sabbatical year of Deuteronomy 15. Every seventh sabbatical year (or once every forty-nine years), jubilee was to be announced—and thus in each fiftieth year, Israel was ordered to practice jubilee (Lev 25:8-11).

The observance of jubilee required several things of the people of Israel. First, during the Year of Jubilee, the land was not to be cultivated but instead was to be allowed to lie fallow and thus restore itself: "You shall not sow, or reap the aftergrowth, or harvest the unpruned vines. For it is a jubilee; it shall be holy to you: you shall eat only what the field itself produces" (Lev 25:11-12). Second, at the jubilee all outstanding debts between Hebrews were to be cancelled, and no interest on a debt could be levied between jubilees (Lev 25:25, 28, 37). Third, all Hebrew slaves and indentured servants were to be set free (Lev 25:39-41).

These three stipulations are, of course, not peculiar to jubilee. You recognize them from our discussion in chapter one as being legislation for each sabbatical year. Since the jubilee is a "sabbatical year writ large," it stands to reason that it would contain within it the regulations of the sabbatical year.

But there is a fourth regulation, peculiar only to the Year of Jubilee. And it is the most important of them all: "In this year of jubilee you shall return, every one of you, to your property. . . . The land shall not be sold in perpetuity, for the land is mine; with me you are but aliens and tenants. . . . In the jubilee, [your land] shall be released, and the property shall be returned" (Lev 25:13, 23, 28). Wealth, during the time of the Jewish nation lay almost entirely in the land. And at jubilee each family was to regain its ancestral land.

At the time of the creation of the jubilee, the assumption was that each Israelite was a descendant of an Israelite who had entered the Promised Land at the time of the conquest under Joshua. As part of that conquest, each Israelite family and tribe had been assigned land. That was their "ancestral land," and no one could take it from them. They could choose to "sell" it for up to forty-nine years for compensation, but at the end of the forty-nine years or until the next jubilee (whichever occurred first), that land had to be returned free of charge to the Israelite family to whom Joshua had originally deeded it. It was their birthright.

Simply put, jubilee was a legislated reversal of fortune! It was Israel's most radical vehicle to redistribute its wealth so that society could be rebalanced and neither wealth nor political power could accumulate in the hands of a self-selected few. *That* was what Jesus was proclaiming when he read Isaiah 61 in the synagogue in Nazareth that sabbath day.

When Jesus proclaimed jubilee time, how did the people hear him, and how did the synagogue (and community) leaders hear him? Luke suggests that Jesus was heard gladly by the people but was heard badly by the synagogue leaders and by the establishment, for they "were filled with rage" (Lk 4:22, 28-30).

At the time of Jesus, the Jewish leaders were essentially concerned about two things. First, like economic, political and religious leaders everywhere, they wanted to keep themselves in a privileged position of power and wealth. Second, as Jews, they were also concerned about obeying the law and calling the people to obey the law—but in ways that would keep themselves in power. This was particularly evident in the way they interpreted the sabbatical year and the jubilee. They personally obeyed and they taught the people to obey only one stipulation of the jubilee—allowing the land to lie fallow—while ignoring the injunctions to forgive debts, release slaves and redistribute wealth.[1] This provided the appearance that they were keeping the law, but in reality the people bearing the greatest economic burden of the jubilee and of sabbatical law were the peasants, artisans and farmers.

So what was Jesus doing by reading Isaiah 61:1-2 in the synagogue and proclaiming, "Today, this Scripture has been fulfilled in your hearing"? In essence he was proclaiming this message: "You wealthy and powerful, as well as the people—you are to keep the entire jubilee and not just one regulation of it. I have come to bring about the setting free of this great people, so that none of us will be rich, none will be poor and all of us will live at shalom with each other." Jesus had come proclaiming a reversal of his entire society, so that wealth, power and religious control would no longer be lodged in the hands of a few while all the rest were thrust into ever deeper poverty. *That is what Jesus meant by "the kingdom of God."*

THE JEWISH WORLD AT THE TIME OF JESUS

To understand these disparate responses of the Jewish leaders and the ordinary people, we must understand Jewish society at the time of Jesus. The Roman Empire dominated the known world during the first three centuries of the Christian era. The Roman Empire was essentially a constellation of small city-states, all of which had pledged allegiance to Rome. Some of these states had been conquered by it. Others had voluntarily come under the Roman eagle. But all had remarkable autonomy. Each city-state had its own appointed or elected city government, its own institutions, authorities, gods and cult. Rome basically allowed home rule, as long as that nation or city gave its allegiance to Rome.[2]

Of course, some of the nations in this empire were more rebellious than others. Such was the case with the Jewish people. Jerusalem, and Judea around it, was under the direct governance of Rome because the nation had remained rebellious and troubled. The remainder of Israel—Galilee and Transjordan—was under the authority of Idumean puppet kings.[3]

Roman law limited the power of the Roman governor or procurator. He essentially had only four responsibilities. First, he was to regulate relations between cities under his protection. Second, he was responsible for guaranteeing the legal privileges of the local government and of Roman citizens within the geographical boundaries of his authority (see Acts 22:24-29). Third, he was to listen to complaints by or against local magistrates (Acts 24:1-9). Finally, the governor or procurator was responsible for forbidding any religious practices that would disturb the Roman peace (Acts 24:5-9). These were the limits of a Roman governor's authority.[4]

How were a nation's political, economic and religious decisions made? Rome left those crucial matters up to that nation's indigenous leadership. The real power of Israel, therefore, was not the Roman governor or procurator. The real power was the native elite who ruled that nation—as long as they remained loyal to Rome!

In Israel, that ruling elite consisted of three groups: the Herodians, the scribes and Pharisees, and the Jerusalem clerical aristocracy.[5] The Herodian nobility was a waning political power during Jesus' adulthood. Once, under the reign of Herod the Great, the Herodians ruled all of Palestine—both Jewish and Gentile areas. But by the time of Jesus' ministry, Herod's successors had been reduced to ruling small territories and had limited rule under Rome. Their power was steadily eroding. By the end of the first century A.D., they would be no more.[6]

The scribes and Pharisees were rapidly rising in power. They were not ordained priests; rather they were experts in the law who built their power on both their knowledge and their adjudication of the Mosaic law. The Pharisees taught the law; the scribes (also called "lawyers" in the Synoptic Gospels) interpreted and adjudicated it. They based their power on the synagogue system throughout Israel, which they controlled. They were the "rabbis" of the synagogues, teaching in every town, village and city, leading sabbath worship each week, and judging all lawsuits and legal disputes (Lk 12:13-14). By seventy years after Jesus' death, they had become the dominant power in Israel.[7]

The Jerusalem clerical aristocracy was by far the most powerful party in Israel at the time of Jesus. It consisted of the priesthood, the elders and the Sadducees, all ruled by the high priest. It was primarily centered in Jerusalem around the temple and its worship, which all Jews were required to attend three times a year. The clerical aristocracy controlled the Sanhedrin, which meant they controlled the legislative and judicial systems of Israel. Because the temple was the major source of income generation and distribution in the nation, this aristocracy also controlled much of the economy. The "landowners," referred to throughout the Gospel narratives, were basically the clerical aristocracy, the Pharisees and scribes, and private entrepreneurs. This aristocracy was fully collaborative with Rome and its administration of justice. The Jerusalem clerical aristocracy would be removed from power by Rome nearly forty years after Jesus' death because of its inability to control the increasing revolutionary movements in Israel (including the Christians).[8]

These three power centers of Israel—the Herodians, the Pharisees and scribes, and the Jerusalem clerical aristocracy—were the true political and economic leaders of Israel. The latter two centers hid their considerable political and economic power behind the controlling regulations, worship and teaching of religion. And the oppressive and overwhelming tax burden of the farmers, artisans and poor peasants of Palestine primarily funded all three of these communities of non-Roman power.

The peasants or farmers made up the vast majority of the Israelite nation—about 80 percent—during the adulthood of Jesus. Virtually no farmers owned their own land; almost all of them worked the land owned by the elite. The artisans or trades people (for example, carpenters, leather workers, tent makers) basically ran small family enterprises and were in significant debt to the elite. The artisans made up about 18 percent of the population. The Herodians, Pharisees, scribes, priesthood, elders, Sadducees and landowners made up only about 2 percent of the Israelite population.[9]

How poor were the peasants? Consider the farmers. Virtually all of their living depended on their annual crop production. But from those harvested crops, the typical farmer had to give 50 percent to the owner of the land. Twenty-five percent went for land taxes to be paid to the Herodian kings and Roman government, and 10 percent went in taxes to the Jewish clerical aristocracy for the running of the temple and the religious apparatus of Israel. In other words, about 85 percent of a typical farmer's annual income went for taxes and liabilities.[10]

Of the remainder, about 3 percent went to the village or town in which the farmer lived in order to be held in reserve for the village to maintain its life, conduct festivals and particularly to use as no-interest loans to neighbors in need. No Israelite would consider or even regret the giving of such money, because he or she might need a loan from that same source someday. That meant the family of the typical Palestinian farmer or artisan had to both live on 12 percent of the annual income they generated *and* purchase the seed and supplies necessary to sustain another year of business. The practical result of such profound poverty was people spiraling deeper and deeper into debt until they were reduced to becoming prostitutes or beggars on the streets.[11]

When Jesus came proclaiming a full—not a truncated—jubilee, it was extremely good news to the farmers, artisans and peasants of Israel. Likewise, it was extremely alarming news to the powerful, who viewed Jesus with a hostility that sprang forth from the very real threat that he posed to them, their power and their wealth.[12]

The mission statement of Jesus found in Luke 4:16-21 is of a full liberation of the people and systems of Israel. It would draw an oppressed and exploited peasantry to him. It would also strike terror into the political, economic and religious elite of Jewish society. But does that mission statement form the thrust of the entire book of Luke, or is it a statement that, once made, Jesus no longer found formative to his ministry? Looking at some pivotal stories in Luke and at the sweep of the book's emphasis clearly answers that question for us.

TWO STORIES OF JUBILEE LIBERATION

A tragic rich man. The story of the *very* rich young ruler (Lk 18:18-25) is not understandable apart from the story that soon follows it—the story of Zacchaeus. Jesus' teaching about wealth and the jubilee in these two stories is profound.[13]

Luke is careful to tell us that this is not simply a rich man. He is "very rich" (Lk 18:23). He possesses enormous wealth, but he is also one who has discovered that his wealth will not bring him happiness. He is an agitated and disturbed young man.

The rich ruler initiates the dialogue by asking Jesus, "Good Teacher, what must I do to inherit eternal life?" Jesus responds by summarizing the law (Lk 18:19-20)—in other words, saying to the man, "You already know what to do. Keep the law, the whole law—and that includes its jubilee regulations." The man, unsatisfied with Jesus' answer, responds, "I have kept all these since my youth," implying that he still feels unsatisfied and separated from God despite his orthodoxy and orthopraxy. Jesus responds with stunning words: "There is still one thing lacking. Sell all that you own and distribute the money to the poor, and you will have treasure in heaven; then come, follow me."

This is an extremely pointed and even harsh response to a person seeking peace with God. In essence Jesus is saying to this young man, "There is one thing that stands between you and God—and that is your money. Your money possesses you more than you possess it. If you really want to be in relationship with God, you need to remove the barrier of your money. This you can do by divesting yourself of all your wealth beyond what you need to sustain your life. Fulfill the jubilee and redistribute your wealth to the poor. If you do this, you will discover an authentic relationship with God. Then, and only then, will you be freed to follow me."

It is particularly significant that in four places in Luke, Jesus links the gaining of eternal life with the handling of money (Lk 10:25-37; 16:19-31; 19:1-10; and in this story). Eternal life is not received simply by faith. It is received by a faith that is demonstrated through the redistribution of our money, following the jubilee and Deuteronomic stipulations regarding its use for the purpose of eliminating poverty.

Predictably the man rejects Jesus' offer. When he does, Jesus says to him (and to all those listening to the conversation), "How hard it is for those who have wealth to enter the kingdom of God! Indeed, it is easier for a camel to go through the eye of a needle than for someone who is rich to enter the kingdom of God" (Lk 18:24-25).

The crowd is amazed at Jesus' words, for they are operating on the assumption that wealth is a sign of God's blessing. For Jesus to say that one's wealth can and often does stand in the way of one's relationship with God and God's kingdom was a direct contradiction of what all Jews had been taught by the religious, political and economic elite (obviously to justify their accumulation of wealth and power). This is revealed in their naive response: "Then [if not the rich and powerful] who can be saved?" (Lk 18:26). Jesus' curt reply is, in essence, "Anyone can be saved whom God chooses to save."

Peter, still not getting it, replies something like this: "Well, if you want to talk dedication, Lord, we've given up everything to follow you. So if the standard of the kingdom is what we've given up rather than what we possess, we should stand very high in the kingdom." Jesus replies, in essence, "Anyone who has sacrificed much for the kingdom of God will be appropriately rewarded by God. But if you want to talk sacrifice, Peter, then understand what commitment to the kingdom is going to cost me (and by implication, all of you who seek to follow me)." Jesus continues, "See, we are going up to Jerusalem, and everything that is written about the Son of Man by the prophets will be accomplished. For he will be handed over to the Gentiles; and he will be mocked and insulted and spat upon. After they have flogged him, they will kill him, and on the third day he will rise again" (Lk 18:31-33).

This is what it means to be committed to the kingdom of God, to follow

Jesus, and to love and serve the Lord. It will not mean wealth and power and prestige; it will mean divestiture, sacrifice and suffering. As Dietrich Bonhoeffer said, "When Christ calls a man, he bids him come and die!"[14]

A transformed rich man. Luke 19:1-10 tells the story of Zacchaeus. Thank God this story is in the Scriptures! Otherwise all we would have is a never-ending story of the rich who are beyond redemption because of their greed. Luke meant this story, which only he told, to work in tandem with the story of the rich young ruler, which all the Synoptic Gospel writers told.

Zacchaeus was a wealthy tax collector in Jericho. Luke calls him a "chief tax collector," which meant he headed a team of subordinates who collected Roman taxes from rich and poor alike. Like all other tax collectors at that time, Zacchaeus could legally charge excess interest on the taxes and thus embezzle significant sums for himself. That he did so is implied in his statement, "If I have defrauded anyone, . . ." Because tax collectors were also "legal crooks," everyone despised them, including the religious and political elite.

Jesus was passing through the city on his way to Jerusalem. As he walked through the crowd gathered to see him, he saw Zacchaeus—and he invited himself to lunch. This was unacceptable because Zacchaeus was considered unclean because of his occupation. But this didn't stop Jesus!

We do not know what transpired in their table conversation. But we do know the outcome. As a result of his having lunch with Jesus, Zacchaeus declared, "Look, half of my possessions, Lord, I will give to the poor; and if I have defrauded anyone of anything, I will pay back four times as much." Jesus responds to Zacchaeus's act, "Today salvation has come to this house. . . . For the Son of Man came to seek out and to save the lost" (Lk 19:8-9).

It is important to notice the order of events here. First Zacchaeus deals with the domination of his money. Then he is free to receive the gift of salvation from Jesus. Salvation came to Zacchaeus's house, not because of his generosity, but because his declaration indicated that his money no longer stood in the way of his relationship with God. Money had been Zacchaeus's god. But he demonstrated that money would no longer control him, because Jesus had touched him. He could happily give it away and could recompense those whom he had cheated. Zacchaeus had removed money from the throne of his life, and now God could claim that throne.

Note the specific commitment Zacchaeus made to redistribute his money.

He went far beyond the jubilee requirement. Leviticus 6:1-5 requires that the person who defrauds reimburses the defrauded person the full amount plus 20 percent interest. Exodus 22:1-4 requires doubling the reimbursement if one defrauded another of livestock. If you had slaughtered or sold the livestock, then you were required to reimburse it fourfold. In essence, Zaccheaus applied the law of slaughtered or sold livestock to his money. By law, he only had to reimburse the amount defrauded plus 20 percent interest. But he reimbursed the defrauded people four times the amount. So Zacchaeus placed upon himself the most stringent demands of the law. Because of what Jesus was doing in his life, he had become a *hilarious* giver (the actual meaning of the Greek word translated "cheerful" in Paul's call to the church to be "cheerful givers"; 2 Cor 9:7). Zacchaeus—and his priorities—had been transformed by a meeting with Jesus.

These stories of the rich young ruler and the transformed tax collector are meant by Luke to be read in tandem. According to Donald Kraybill, "In the first story economic concerns stagnate faith. In the second story faith drives the economic agenda. Here are two contradictory responses to the gospel, opposite reactions to the poor. On the one hand, good theology, no jubilee, condemnation. On the other hand, scant theology, jubilee, salvation."[15]

These stories of two rich men present a common message. The first story demonstrates clearly how the rich are so captured by their wealth that they cannot even act on their own salvation. The Zacchaeus story demonstrates how the rich oppressor can be delivered from the control of his wealth through his repentant response to the very people he has oppressed. Thus Jesus intentionally links a person's salvation to his or her acts of social justice. In these and other stories in Luke we see amplified Jesus' call for the restoration of the full jubilee in Israel's life and practice.

WHAT IS THE GOSPEL OF LUKE ALL ABOUT?

In the Gospel of Luke, Jesus is committed to the bringing in of the kingdom of God (the shalom community). This kingdom will bring in its wake a grand reversal in which poverty and systems of domination will be eliminated and humanity will become all that God intended it to be. This reversal will occur through the intervention of Jesus as the one bringing about jubilee. Through his life and ministry, his empowering of people, his confrontation of the systems, his suffering, death and resurrection, Jesus will set the stage for the resurrection of humanity into "the world as God intended."

Evidence for the above assertion is displayed throughout the Gospel of Luke. The focus of Luke is on demonstrating that Jesus is a man for the people—the "little ones" of the earth who hold no political, economic, social or religious power, who are marginalized and often oppressed by the systems of societal power. To them Jesus brings the good news of a new and just kingdom—the kingdom of God.

The clearest indication that Luke's Gospel is committed to the jubilee and its liberation of the poor is found in Luke's handling of the Beatitudes. In the Sermon on the Mount, Matthew records Jesus as saying, "Blessed are the poor in spirit, for theirs is the kingdom of heaven." Again, "Blessed are those who hunger and thirst for righteousness, for they will be filled" (Mt 5:3, 6). But Luke remembers Jesus' words differently. He records Jesus as saying, "Blessed are you who are poor, for yours is the kingdom of God. Blessed are you who are hungry now, for you will be filled. Blessed are you who weep now, for you will laugh" (Lk 6:20-21).

Then Luke records Jesus continuing with words that do not appear in Matthew at all: "Woe to you who are rich, for you have received your consolation. Woe to you who are full now, for you will be hungry. Woe to you who are laughing now, for you will mourn and weep" (Lk 6:24-25). There will be a great reversal, Jesus proclaims in Luke. For the day will come when wealth and food will be redistributed, and those who currently enjoy the bounty of life will be destitute while those who are now oppressed and exploited will be on top—all because the wealthy and powerful would not share their wealth.

Clearly the content of the Gospel of Luke is consistent with Jesus' commission in Luke 4:18-19. Those stories are the lived-out reality of Jesus' mission call. His commission is to bring good news to the poor, to seek the release of the captives, to bring sight to the blind, to work for the liberation of the oppressed and to insist upon the full implementation of jubilee so that wealth is effectively redistributed and poverty eliminated. According to Luke, Jesus' work was the work of the Messiah reestablishing jubilee throughout Israel and perhaps even the world.

And that to which Jesus is called, his followers are also called. When

Jesus proclaimed in Luke, "The kingdom of God is among you," he was indicating that God had already planted the seeds of the kingdom both *in us* and *in our midst* (the double meaning of the Greek in Lk 17:21). So it then becomes our responsibility to carry on the ministry he initiated. "Whenever you enter a town and its people welcome you, . . . cure the sick who are there, and say to them, 'The kingdom of God has come near to you'" (Lk 10:8-9). And that is the message of Luke's companion work, the Acts of the Apostles, which demonstrates the Christian community living out the jubilee regulations in their life together (see Acts 2:1-47; 4:32—5:16; 11:29-30; compare 1 Cor 16:1-4; 2 Cor 9:1-15; Gal 2:1-10) and carrying the good news of God's kingdom throughout Israel (Acts 1:1—8:3), Samaria (Acts 8:4-25), the Gentile world (Acts 8:26—21:16) and finally to Rome (Acts 21:17—28:31).

JESUS IN MATTHEW, MARK AND JOHN

Each of the four Gospels presents a powerful Jesus. But each Gospel writer presents his own particular nuance of Jesus according to the particular agenda of that author.[16]

The Gospel of Matthew presents Jesus as the *marginalized Messiah.*[17] It focuses on reaching the Jews of the first century with the claims of Jesus the Messiah. Toward that end, the author stresses the Jewish foundation of Christianity in everything he writes. But Matthew also portrays Jesus as a marginalized Messiah. Jesus is the one on the outskirts, among the rejected ones and himself rejected, bringing a salvation that comes from the margins and not the center.

In Matthew, it is the political, economic and religious systems that reject Jesus both throughout the story and at his crucifixion, seeking to marginalize him (Mt 27:41-43). But it is only in Matthew that the author tells us these leaders of Israel *knew Jesus rose from the dead* and, rather than admit their guilt, *cover up that resurrection* (Mt 28:11-15). Those in power are so committed to holding on to their power that they lie and protect their interests. They choose to "save their life" and thereby "lose it" (Mt 16:25). So with that action, the "mainstream" Jewish systems become marginalized in the Gospel of Matthew, and the marginalized Jesus and his church become the center of the world.

The Gospel of Mark presents Jesus as the *radical rabbi*.[18] Likely written in that moment between Israel's seemingly successful revolt against Rome in A.D. 66 and its total destruction by the Roman military machine in A.D. 70, Mark reflects the choice before all Jews. Do they remain loyal to Rome and its Jewish representatives (chief priests, elders, Pharisees, Sadducees), or do they join with the Zealots in revolt? Mark suggests that Jesus' life, ministry, death and resurrection call the church to a third way—to a "radical" approach to the world and its institutions that goes far beyond either the maintenance of the status quo or revolution. For to be radical means that one goes to the root (from the Latin *radix*, or "root") both in one's social analysis and in one's actions.

The Gospel of John presents Jesus as the *countercultural Christ*.[19] In its magnificent prologue, the writer of John lays out the intent of his book. That prologue proclaims that God is "tabernacling" his Word among humanity in one human being so that we might become God's people, living out "grace and truth" (Jn 1:17) in both our private and public lives and in the very ways we carry out the political, economic and religious functions of our society. The Mosaic law and its systems, designed to "tabernacle" God, had become the oppressive means of the elite to maintain their power while holding the populace in economic, political and religious slavery. Now, rather, "grace and truth come through Jesus Christ." Thus the remainder of the Gospel of John is a demonstration through the life and teachings, death and resurrection of Jesus Christ of the authenticity of what John has proposed in the prologue. And it demonstrates that authenticity against the landscape of the horrendous oppression of the Jewish and Roman systems that has driven these systems beyond redemption.

What would happen if the church would reclaim for itself the Jesus of Matthew, Mark, Luke and John? How would the church be different if it believed that Jesus worked for the transformation of both people *and* their society? What would happen if we believed that God's work of salvation was as big as the totality of sin—corporate as well as individual; social, economic and political as well as spiritual—and that Christ had come to die for all of that world? How would the church in your city be different if it saw itself as working with Christ for the building of your city's shalom? And what could Christian people like you accomplish to right the wrongs in your city, if they could see such work as being the logical extension of the work that their Lord and Savior had come to do? What would happen if we really were to take Jesus seriously?

4

WHAT SHOULD
THE CHURCH BE ABOUT?

WHAT IS THE WORK OF THE CHURCH to which the Bible calls us? Let's look at one biblical answer.

What Ezekiel prophesied would happen did indeed happen. The southern kingdom of Judah was conquered by the Babylonian empire. The political, economic and religious systems of the nation collapsed, and with them, the nation. The city of Jerusalem was burned to the ground and the temple destroyed. The nation's leaders were dragged off as captives to the city of Babylon by the invading king, Nebuchadnezzar. There in the city of their captors, these former Israelite leaders began to despair that God would ever deliver them.

It was to those despairing, grieving captives that a letter came from the prophet Jeremiah. And his advice to those exiles is a word we need to hear as we seek to be God's faithful people in our time. That letter—and its advice—now appears in Jeremiah 29:4-13:

> Thus says the LORD of hosts, the God of Israel, to all the exiles whom I have sent into exile from Jerusalem to Babylon: Build houses and live in them; plant gardens and eat what they produce. Take wives and have sons and daughters; take wives for your sons, and give your daughters in marriage, that they may bear sons and daughters; multiply there, and do not decrease. But seek the

[shalom] of the city where I have sent you into exile, and pray to the LORD on its behalf, for in its [shalom] you will find your [shalom]. . . . For thus says the LORD: Only when Babylon's seventy years are completed will I visit you, and I will fulfill to you my promise and bring you back to this place. For surely I know the plans I have for you, says the LORD, plans for your [shalom] and not for harm, to give you a future with hope. (Jer 29:4-7, 10-11)

SEEKING THE SHALOM OF THE CITY

"Only when Babylon's seventy years are completed will I . . . bring you back to [Jerusalem]." Yahweh's initial promise to the Israelite political, economic and religious leaders in Babylonian exile seems a harsh promise. Through this prophecy, God tells the Israelite leaders they will remain in exile for seventy years—in other words, a lifetime! They will not be restored to their precious city of Jerusalem. Likely neither will their children. Only in their grandchildren lies the hope that Israel will once again be restored to its land.

How then can God say to them, "I know the plans I have for you . . . plans for your [shalom] and not for harm, to give you a future with hope" (Jer 29:11)? What kind of future is God giving to them as they live and die in captivity? How is such a life in slavery "a future with hope" and free of "harm"?

Though they will remain a lifetime and die in Babylonian exile, God's plan for these captive Israelite leaders is meant for their good. It was as if God were saying to the Israelites, "It is my plan that you are here. And I promise you that I will bless you in this place—this foreign city. I will make you a rich blessing to all around you, for the promise I give to you is realized as you live out the plan I have for you here in this city of your exile." Here, according to Jeremiah, is the good news in the midst of dark news. Here is God's promise for us called to be the church today.

IN THE CITY BY CIRCUMSTANCE OR CALL?

"Seek the [shalom] of the city where I have *sent you into exile.*" The English words *sent you into exile* are actually the translation of a single Hebrew word that has a double meaning.[1] It can rightfully be translated "exile," and it can also be translated "sent." Thus it is reasonable to assume that in the use of this one Hebrew word, Jeremiah is seeking to communicate two distinct ideas to his Hebrew brothers and sisters in Babylon. He is, in essence, saying to the Israelites, "You are in captivity because your nation was defeated, your army destroyed, your city burned, and you were clapped into chains and marched across the desert into Babylonian exile. That is your *circumstance*. But you are also in captivity because I, the Lord your God, sent you there. You are in Babylon because I need my people in this wicked city. That is your *call from God.*"

Here is God's promise—not only for Israelite captives but also for all of us called to be the church wherever we may be. We are not in our community simply because of our circumstances—because we were born here, or moved here to take a job or to get an education or to accompany our spouse. We are in this community because the Lord our God has called us here, sent us here and needs us here! We are in our city or town or university or mission station by the intentional will of God acted out through the particularity of our circumstances.

Therefore, as God's sent people, what are we called to be and do in the place we are planted? We are called to the very same task as were the Israelite captives in the city of Babylon twenty-six hundred years ago: "[You are to] seek the [shalom] of the city where I have sent you into exile, . . . for in its [shalom] you will find your [shalom]" (Jer 24:7). Our calling as God's people in whatever situation God might have us is to seek that community's shalom.

WHERE SHALOM IS TO BE SOUGHT

Note where we are to seek shalom. It is not in Jerusalem—the "city of God." It is in Babylon—the "city of Satan." This statement was utterly shocking to the Israelites—totally unthinkable![2] The Israelites were called to seek God's shalom in the midst of Babylon. And they would not experience personal shalom as long as Babylon was not a city at peace within itself.

What made this statement such a revolutionary one was that Babylon was the ultimate symbol of evil to Israel. In the Israelite culture, Babylon was a virtual synonym for depravity. In Genesis 11:1-9 the Tower of Babel (the Hebrew form of the name Babylon) is the symbolic place of the "confusion of language" where the unity of the world is shattered. Throughout the Bible's historical books and the prophets, Babylon is pictured as evil (see 2 Kings 20:12-19; 24:10—25:30; Is 13—14; 47—48; Jer 25:8-14; Acts 7:43). And in Revelation 17—18 the elder John gives the name Babylon to human civilization living in defiance of God and practicing a politics of oppression and an economics of greed and exploitation.

To Israel, Babylon is the epitome of the wickedest and darkest of cities. Jeremiah is saying that, precisely in the midst of such wickedness and darkness, God's people are to work for shalom. Shalom is not to be sought among God's people but among those who most reject God. And why? Because God loves all Babylons and can transform them only by sending God's people there, even against their will.

In fact Jeremiah takes it a step further. He states in verse seven, "For in its [shalom] you will find your [shalom]." Even those who are in relationship with God and within the embrace of a godly community can never fully know peace for themselves if their city does not experience peace. So God sends God's people into the darkest areas of human society to be ambassadors for shalom there.

What Is Our "City"?

But what does it mean to seek the city's peace?[3] When Jeremiah instructs the exiled Israelites to seek the shalom of Babylon, it is clear where he wants them to be at work. But what does "city to which God has sent you" mean for us today?

When the biblical writers speak of a city, they mean that geographical area and its people contained within the city's walls. When Christians now speak of the city, they most often mean the inner city—that portion of the city that is physically old, that is made up of the city's poor and that contains people who are of a racial or ethnic group that is in the nation's minority, who speak a language other than English, who are poorly educated and/or who are extremely transient. However, that is an inadequate understanding of city for the twenty-first century.

A city is an entire metropolitan area that is interwoven economically, by transit (both public and private), by public communication and by identification. Thus Los Angeles doesn't simply consist of the political entity named Los Angeles; it is 124 "cities" tied together by economics, expressways, rail lines, four international airports, common television and radio stations and a common identity as "Los Angeles." It consists of the entirety of one county and portions of four other counties covering a geographical area wider than the state of Indiana. It consists of very wealthy areas (Beverly Hills, San Marino, Santa Monica) and very poor areas (East Los Angeles, Compton, Pomona). Fifty-two of its 124 member cities contain "inner cities," slums and even squatter settlements. And it has over twenty downtowns! A similar litany can be recited on any major metropolis in the United States today.

It is very easy for the church to say, "We are not inner-city, and therefore we are not city." That is simply not true, and to make that claim severely limits the effectiveness of the church in seeking the welfare of its city. As the body of Christ and as Christians, we are responsible to bring shalom both to our own neighborhood and to our entire metropolis. So whatever "Babylon" may be for you, God calls you to seek its welfare—whether it is an inner-city neighborhood, a wealthy suburb, a small town or a university campus.

And what does it mean to work for our city's shalom? It is intriguing to note how different versions of the Bible translate the word *shalom* in Jeremiah 29:7. It is variously translated as "peace," "prosperity," "welfare," "good."[4] Each translation seeks to capture the rich implications of this command, for our task is to work for the peace *and* the prosperity *and* the welfare *and* the good of all the people, the systems and structures, and even the principalities and powers of our city. It means that nothing is outside the purview, concern or commitment of the church, whether it is political, economic, religious, social, cultural, environmental or spiritual, whether it is in the public domain or in the private. The essential task of the church is to work for its society's shalom—to work for the full and total transformation of all the people, forces and structures with the love of God.

WORKING FOR THE SHALOM OF YOUR CITY

How are we to work for the shalom of our city? As God's ambassadors to Babylon, how were the Jewish leaders to seek the shalom of that evil city? Jeremiah suggested to them three elements that need to be in their ministry in order to seek Babylon's peace—and the New Testament would add a fourth.

Become God's presence. First, Jeremiah instructs us, become God's presence in your society: "Build houses and live in them; plant gardens and eat what they produce. Take wives and have sons and daughters; take wives for your sons, and give your daughters in marriage, that they may bear sons and daughters; multiply there, and do not decrease" (Jer 29:5-6). In other words,

"Don't isolate yourself from the rest of the Babylonian community and create a Jewish ghetto. Enter fully into the life of that city. Get a job and enter into its economy. Buy a house or rent an apartment. Become Yahweh-lovers who love the city's people and corporate life. Weep with those who weep. Laugh with those who laugh. And by so doing, become God's presence in the society to which I have called you."

What Jeremiah and many others in Scripture are saying is that the people of God must become *incarnational*. You are to become the presence of God in your city, because many people will only know God through their experience with you.

Pray for the city. Second, pray for your community. "Pray to the Lord on [your city's] behalf," Jeremiah instructs the Israelite captives (Jer 29:7). Pray for each other, Paul instructs us, both as individual Christians and as the church, "that your love may overflow more and more with knowledge and full insight, . . . so that in the day of Christ you may be pure and blameless, having produced the harvest of righteousness that comes through Jesus Christ" (Phil 1:9-11).

Prayer only for people you know and love and for the community of faith does not fulfill the ministry of prayer to which we are called. We are also to pray for the political, economic and values-producing systems of our city and the world, and for the people who are in the service of and provide leadership to those systems—*by name*. There are many means by which one may pray for a city, including, of course, individual prayer. But it is far more important to pray as God's people together. Such praying might take the form of prayer-walks, civic prayer vigils to combat violence, concerts of prayer, prayers for spiritual deliverance and intercession for the city, prayers confronting the powers—or simply congregational prayers each Sunday for the systems of their city and their representatives. However this is done, God's people must pray regularly and systematically for their city's leaders, systems, and the principalities and powers behind those systems.

Practice your faith through action. Third, we are to practice our faith by working for social justice and shalom. "*Work* for the [shalom] of your city," Jeremiah instructs the Babylonian exiles (Jer 29:7 NLT). But how are we to do that?

First, we are to undertake *ministries of mercy* and seek to serve the needs of the poor. Jesus would call us to feed the hungry, give drink to the thirsty, welcome the stranger, clothe the naked, care for the sick, visit the prisoner, for "just as you did it to one of the least of these who are members of my family, you did it to me" (Mt 25:31-40). Ministries of mercy are carried out today through the provision of *social services.*

Second, we are to be *advocates for the powerless.* It is the job of God's people to "stand in the breach" and defend the cause of the poor, the powerless and the marginalized before the "principalities and powers" of the city and state. An excellent example of that ministry of advocacy is seen in Jeremiah 22:13-17, when, on behalf of the people, the prophet confronts the king for his lavish lifestyle in the face of such intense poverty.

But there is a third ministry of practice to which God's people are called: *community development*—working with and mobilizing the poor to provide needed community services for themselves. Isaiah stated it quite clearly when he called God's people to work with all society to pressure for health care that would guarantee long life and the elimination of infant mortality, adequate and affordable housing for all, fulfilling work for everyone, the elimination of unemployment, and harmony among ethnic, racial and national groups (Is 65:19-25).

Proclaim the good news. Fourth, the New Testament insists that an essential role of the church in its work of shalom is that of proclamation. Paul put the task quite directly: "Everyone who calls on the name of the Lord shall be saved. But how are they to call on one in whom they have not believed? And how are they to believe in one of whom they have never heard? And how are they to hear without someone to proclaim him?" (Rom 10:13-14). An essential task of the church is to proclaim Christ to any who will listen, for only in that way will they believe.

But proclamation is to be made to more than people. Paul tells us that "through the church the wisdom of God in its rich variety might now be made known to the rulers and authorities in the heavenly places" (Eph 3:10). It is the responsibility of the church to proclaim God's prophetic and reconciling word to the political, economic and values-producing systems of our society and to the leaders of those structures.

Presence, prayer, practice, proclamation—these are the shalom-building ministries of the church in society. They are not optional. We do not have the right to choose between them. All of them together make up the substance of the work of God's people for our society's transformation. These four ministries make up the *essential* work of the church and are the *strategic* work of the church. But, frankly, neither in today's global urban world nor in the biblical world are or were these four ministries *sufficient*.

Why are they not sufficient? Simply because none of these four by itself, nor all of them together, are powerful enough to pressure the giant political, economic, educational, media/entertainment, religious, social service or health care institutions and their massive bureaucracies to practice shalom. If these are not enough, what else is needed?

ACTION THAT IS SUFFICIENT FOR CHANGING SYSTEMS

What more must the church do to truly make a difference in today's world? The answer is found in one of the most disturbing statements made by Jesus: "I came to bring fire to the earth, and how I wish it were already kindled! I have a baptism with which to be baptized, and what stress I am under until it is completed! Do you think that I have come to bring peace to the earth? No, I tell you, [I have not come to bring peace] but rather division!" (Lk 12:49-51). What does Jesus mean by this? Let me get at the truth of this disturbing statement by describing an event from my ministry experience.

We were about to begin a meeting of the governing board of the church I served in a large American city, and I was waiting for the last elders to assemble. Suddenly the door opened with a bang and John, one of our elders who lived in the neighborhood, stalked into the room, obviously deeply agitated. "I can't believe it," he said. "I have just been turned down by our community bank for a housing renovation loan."

We were as shocked as John. He was a top executive in his corporation, a man with considerable income and equity, as well as thirty years in the community and a reputation for involvement in community affairs. On what grounds could he possibly be rejected for a loan?

"That's strange," said another elder who also lived in the community. "I was turned down for a home renovation loan only the other day." A third elder and then a fourth spoke up. They too had been turned down for home purchase or remodeling loans in our neighborhood over the past three years. What was going on?

I immediately became suspicious, so at the next meeting of our ministerial association, I shared with the other clergy the strange discovery at that meeting of my church elders. The other clergy all promised to check with their respective church lay leaders as well.

At the next meeting a month later, the results were gathered. *Every* lay leader living in this urban community who had requested a home purchase or improvement loan over the past three years had been rejected for that loan. With that news, we spread out into the community and soon discovered that we could not find a single homeowner who had applied for a home-improvement or home-purchase loan over the past three years and had actually been granted one.

We began investigating the reason, and it soon surfaced. In this declining neighborhood, the bank and fiduciary institutions, a major insurance company, several major contractors, and the city government were involved in a conspiracy to redline the community so that property values would plummet, the community would rapidly decline, buildings could be purchased at basement prices and the area could then be condemned and eventually rebuilt with luxury condominiums and apartment houses at great profit to the bank and developers.[5]

The pastors and lay leaders from the twenty-three churches gathered. The very future of our neighborhood was at stake. What were the churches going to do? We considered together possible alternatives. One was simply to seek to preserve and sustain our congregations as loving fellowships of believers. In other words, we would continue to be a *presence* in the community until the city claimed eminent domain and purchased the church sites. If we did that, we might temporarily sustain our churches, but we would not stop the destruction of our community.

A second suggestion was that we might hold prayer meetings throughout our churches to pray for our community. By doing this, we would be carrying on a ministry of *prayer*. But we concluded that prayer without action would be insufficient to stop this willful pillaging of the community.

A third alternative we considered was that we could evangelize in the community. In other words, we could all participate jointly in a ministry of *proclamation.* That might bring a number of individuals in the community to Christ, but it would not stop the community-destroying policy of those redlining political and economic systems.

A fourth possibility we considered was to provide community services to the people of our neighborhood who became victims of the systems' intentional war of attrition on our community. That is, we could carry on a ministry of *practicing our faith through social services.* But we realized such an approach would not stop the systems from destroying the community.

Rather than doing community services, we could enter into a ministry of *practice through advocacy.* We preachers could appear before city council and advocate the cause of the community. But we quickly realized that this kind of action would be insufficient. The council would simply deny our allegations and dismiss us.

Still another way we could carry out a ministry of *practice* was *through community development.* We could mobilize the community to take care of itself: clean up the streets the city's sanitation department was neglecting; pick up the garbage and trash the city wasn't picking up; police the streets ourselves. But we quickly realized that mobilizing the people to develop our community, while an important task, would not encourage the city and fiduciary institutions to abandon their plan. In fact, if we were to take on the work the city was legally responsible for providing (like garbage removal, sanitation, policing, infrastructure maintenance), we would allow the city to avoid its legal responsibility to our neighborhood.

We finally came to the inevitable alternative. We realized we had to directly confront those greedy political and economic leaders with sufficient people power so that they would *have* to listen. That is, if we were to save our community and our churches from literal destruction, we would have to learn to use *power.*

That filled many of the pastors with dread because as good Christians we had always been taught to obey the systems, not to confront them. But we were also faced with the certain destruction of our neighborhood, and eventually of our churches, if we did nothing.

Whereas prayer, presence, proclamation, and the practices of social services, advocacy and community development are essential and strategic elements of the church's ministry in today's society, they are not sufficient.

There has to be a better way, and that way is a clearly biblical way that is often ignored: the intentional use of power by God's people.

What is the biblical use of power? Well, what do you call it when Moses appears before Pharaoh and demands, "Thus says the LORD: Let my people go" (Ex 8:1)? What is it that David demonstrates against Goliath and the Philistines—and even against an ineffective Saul? What was Elijah using against Ahab, or Daniel against Nebuchadnezzar, or Nehemiah as he organized the people against the political and economic power of the Persian governor Sanballat and the economic powerhouse Tobiah? What was it that Jesus was using in his miracles, in his continuing confrontations of the Pharisees, Sadducees, priests and scribes, and in his death and resurrection? What was Paul doing when he defeated the Jewish leaders who sought to persecute the church, convinced the Christian leaders to aggressively seek the evangelization of the Gentiles and taught passive resistance to Rome? All of these people understood power. And all of these people were not afraid to use power.

THE NATURE OF POWER

What is power?[6] *Power is the ability, capacity and willingness of a person, a group of people or an institution to act.* Each word of that definition is important. *Ability* means having the knowledge to act and the skills to carry out that action. *Capacity* means having the resources to act, whether those resources are human, legal, material or financial. *Willingness* means the commitment to act. The ability, capacity and willingness to act is neither good nor bad in itself. What makes power constructive or destructive is how it is used and for what purpose it is used.

There are two essential types of power. The first is *unilateral*. That is the kind used by the fiduciary institutions, government and contractors in the illustration I presented above. Unilateral power is basically *power over* a people. There are two types of unilateral power. *Dominating power* is the "lowest" form, exercised by a government or group through the force of guns and physical intimidation. It is the tyrannical use of power. It was dominating unilateral power against which Ezekiel wrote. A second form of unilateral power is *constitutional power*. This is a "higher," or more sophisticated, form of power than dominating power. But it is still essentially unilateral in nature. Constitutional power is power over people as defined by the law. It tends to be highly structured and hierarchical, with responsibility being delegated by the people to those who hold power. This was the kind of power exercised by Pilate in his trial of Jesus as he played the role of a Roman judge.

The other essential type of power is *relational power*. Whereas unilateral power is power *over* a constituency, relational power is *power with*. Therefore it is a higher form of participatory power than either dominating or constitutional power. There are two types of relational power, the first being *mutual power*, which exists when two people or groups hold equal power. Rather than trying to enhance their own power at the expense of the other party, however, mutual powers will respect each other's influence and position. It is therefore a negotiating exercise of power. A biblical example of mutual power was that exercised by David and Jonathan toward each other. Jonathan had power as the son of the king; David's power was based on his military acumen and popularity. Both men could have acted destructively toward each other, and Israel would have suffered. Instead, because they loved each other, both used their mutual power to strengthen and secure Israel.

The second type of relational power is *reciprocal power*. This is the deepest form of relational power. It is one in which the people understand that both parties or forces can benefit from power decisions if they authentically share those decisions. Therefore reciprocal power is truly shared power in which each party is of equal strength, is equally participative in the decision-making process and is committed not to its private or exclusive good but to the common good. This was the type of power presented in Deuteronomy as the base for a relational culture that resulted in justice, an equitable distribution of goods and the elimination of poverty. If power is the ability to act, relational power is the capacity to organize people and their institutions (churches, social clubs, schools, unions and so on) around common values and relationships so they can act together as one to bring about the change they desire.

But are unilateral power and relational power truly the only kinds of power in the world? What about spiritual power, the ongoing work of the Holy Spirit in the lives and actions of Christians, which manifests itself in words, deeds or signs of power? Yes, there are Spirit-filled words, deeds and signs of power throughout the Bible. But they are not acts of power distinct from unilateral or relational power. Rather, those acts of Spirit-led or demonic uses of power are either relational or unilateral in nature.

Essentially Yahweh is described in Scripture as a relational God, yearning for relationship both with the people and society he has created. Even the words used for God are relational in nature—Father, Son, Spirit—and God's work in and through us is described in relational terms—*hesed, agapē* love, *phileō* (brotherly) love, grace, truth, covenant. Evil, on the other hand, is described unilaterally—whether it is the evil of people, society, the demonic or the Evil One. The work of Satan is seen as a work of domination, of power over people and nations, with evil as its primary intent.

Now this is not to say that all relational power is always good and all unilateral power is evil. When carried out by humanity, relational power can become manipulative and destructive; that is why the oppressed tend to become the new oppressors once power is gained. But relational power is never evil or destructive when in the hands of God. Our responsibility as children of God is to use relational power in ways that will be both pleasing to God and transforming of each other.

Jesus' confrontations with the leaders of Israel present us with an intriguing study of Jesus' use of power (Mt 21:23—22:46). These confrontations include stories of Jesus in verbal combat with the chief priests and elders, other stories of Jesus arguing with the Pharisees, and one story of a verbal battle with the Sadducees (Mt 21:25, 31, 43; 22:13-14).

In the first story, on the question of authority Jesus outsmarts the priests and elders by asking, "Did the baptism of John come from heaven, or was it of human origin?" In the next story, he confronts these religious leaders with the truth that "the tax collectors and the prostitutes are going into the kingdom of God ahead of you." In the third story, he tells the parable of the wicked tenants and declares, "The kingdom of God will be taken away from you and given to a people that produces the fruits of the kingdom." In the fourth confrontation, Jesus tells the parable of the wedding banquet and describes those who have been chosen (these leaders of Israel) as being bound "hand and foot, and throw[n] . . . into the outer darkness, where there will be weeping and gnashing of teeth." He concludes, "Many are called, but few are chosen."

With the priests and elders defeated, it is now the Pharisees and the Herodians who take Jesus on (Mt 21:15-22). They attempt to trap Jesus with the question, "Is it lawful to pay taxes to the emperor, or not?" But Jesus out-smarts them by responding, "Give . . . to the emperor the things that are the emperor's, and to God the things that are God's" (Mt 22:21).

The Sadducees are next. They seek to trick him in a question about the resurrection (Mt 22:23-33). But again Jesus outsmarts them. Finally the Pharisees regroup and confront Jesus once more (Mt 22:34-40) by seeking to catch him on the issue, "Which commandment in the law is the greatest?" But Jesus brilliantly combines both commandments into one. Finally he goes into the offensive and proves to them from Scripture that the Messiah is the ruler even over the systems (Mt 22:41-45).

How is power being used in this pericope? Consider the power of the priests, elders, Pharisees, Herodians and Sadducees. The power they are ex-ercising is unilateral power. They are using the authority of their office, their wealth, their political and religious clout, and the military authority of Rome to seek either to defeat Jesus or to discredit him. They are exercising domi-nating unilateral power.

Jesus, on the other hand, is using relational power. But how can we argue that Jesus is using relational power? After all, he is not being very "relational" with these Israelite leaders; in this story he is being brutal.

How did Jesus use relational power? That question is answered through a very intriguing refrain that occurs throughout this pericope. It appears in Matthew 21:26, 45-46 and 22:33, and is captured in the Gospel writer's commentary, "The chief priests and the Pharisees . . . wanted to arrest him, but they feared the crowds, because they regarded him as a prophet" (Mt 21:45-46). The political, economic and religious leaders of Israel saw Jesus as a threat to their domination of the people. But they didn't dare arrest him, because they were afraid the crowd would rebel, a riot would ensue, and Rome would remove these leaders from their privileged positions. Jesus had used relational power to build such a profound and deep relationship with the crowd that the people had become the *protectors* of Jesus. (Incidentally, this explains why the Israelite leaders arrested Jesus at night, while he was virtually alone in a garden, and during the Feast of the Passover when every-one else would be in their homes celebrating.)

The response the religious leaders are seeking from the people is compli-ance. In essence all of the arguments they pose to Jesus can be summarized in their question of him, "By what authority are you doing these things?" (Mt 21:23). Their plan was to expose Jesus as a charlatan and disgrace him before the people. By doing so, the Israelite elite hoped to communicate to the people that the only reasonable and rational course of action was for the people to accept the restraints of living under the current leadership. They seem to be saying, "God has designed fundamental laws for society to operate as it does, and this man keeps defying those laws. So don't be fools and follow him. Instead accept the inevitable because it is God-ordained."

Of course the elite hadn't planned on being bested in each argument by Jesus. It was they who were made to look foolish. And the systems of Israelite society, rather than looking like fundamental laws ordained by God, were exposed by Jesus as the power-grabbing, politically compromising and greed-dominated systems they actually were.

Through his use of reciprocal relational power ("You people protect me from the elite, and I'll expose the elite for what they truly are"), Jesus defeated the Israelite elite in debate. By doing so, he destabilized the power equation. The people were no longer willing to remain in compliance with the systems. At this point the people are called by Jesus to move beyond compliance to a higher level of power. Jesus calls his followers to embrace the power level of commitment to him (Mt 23:34-35; 24:36-44; 25:1-46), being filled with the Holy Spirit and assuming the building of God's shalom kingdom. But he fears—in fact he *knows*—that a majority of them will settle for indifference or conformity to custom as the systems reassert their authority (Mt 23:37-39; 24:32-51).

And what will the systems do? With the power equation destabilized by Jesus, the systems desire to move the level of consent by the people down to the lowest level—acquiescence. Their motivation in doing this is their fear that the opposite will happen—that rather than accepting the new imposition of priestly authority, the people will rebel. Therefore they decide that Jesus must be eliminated as quietly and as quickly as possible, for only in this way can the Israelite elite reestablish their authority, receive the acquiescence of the people and once again stabilize the situation (Mt 23:29-36; 26:1-5).

Of course, Jesus can see where all this will lead—to the betrayal of the people by Israel's political, economic and religious elite (23:1-36), the inevitable retaliation by Rome, the destruction of the temple, the persecution and profound suffering of the people, and the elimination of the nation of Israel (24:1-28). Once again, the people will be the victims—and all because the Israelite elite will not recognize what God is doing in their midst, and repent and embrace the shalom community that God would freely give to them.

THE END OF THE STORY

This examination of power brings us back to the story I shared earlier about the discovery of redlining in the urban neighborhood in which I served as a pastor. We found that the community's banks, fiduciary institutions, city government and contractors were involved in a major conspiracy to redline our community as the first step to destroying it, razing its housing, moving out its people, and building housing and an infrastructure for the very wealthy. So what did we do?

We decided to confront those systems. We began with a power analysis of all the institutions participating in the redlining. We quickly realized that the most vulnerable of these institutions was also the most pivotal, because without its participation in refusing loans, the community would not rapidly decline. The bank and the bank's president became our target because the bank was most dependent on maintaining a positive neighborhood image and keeping the goodwill of its customers.

Having selected the bank as our target, we planned a strategy to convince its president to abandon the redlining. We began our campaign to implement that strategy, working behind the scenes for many months to recruit the church and community cooperation necessary to make our confrontation of the bank a success. Because the pastors had through the years built solid relationships of trust throughout the neighborhood, it wasn't difficult to recruit such cooperation.

Finally the day came for the confrontation. A carefully selected team of well-known and influential neighborhood, religious and community business leaders met with the president of the bank. We presented to him the redlining we had uncovered and the bank's involvement in it. Of course he denied everything, but when we showed him our evidence—even the architectural drawings of the proposed apartment and condominium complex and the shopping mall—he stopped his denial.

We then got to the point of the meeting. "We understand," we said, "that the bank has a committee of five that makes the decision on each requested home purchase or renovation loan."

"That is correct," he confirmed.

"We demand," we said, "that six community representatives be appointed to serve on this committee, that the bank not increase its representation of five, and that we select those six community representatives."

"I can't agree to that," the president replied. "That would give the community control over the granting of loans. That would be an abdication of the bank's fiscal responsibility."

"We realize that," we said, "but we are unwilling to have our community destroyed before our eyes."

"Well, I won't do it," the president stated categorically.

"That decision is within your prerogative as bank president," we replied. "But before you make your final decision, it is important that you recognize the full consequences of that decision."

We then spread upon his desk legally binding and notarized papers in which each of our twenty-three churches had agreed to withdraw our respective funds and close our respective accounts. Twenty-one of the churches had agreed to withdraw major investments in the bank worth tens of millions, and many of the businesses and thousands of the bank's customers (most of whom were parishioners of our churches) had all agreed to withdraw all their funds and close their accounts—and all of these withdrawals would occur on a single day!

Threatened with the likely financial collapse of his bank, the president agreed to our demands. He signed a binding agreement between the bank and the community organization, we named the six to the committee, and house purchase and renovation loans began flowing into that community. Faced with the effective defection of the bank from the redlining conspiracy, the other parties withdrew. Our community had been saved by the willingness of that neighborhood's churches to confront those who intended to destroy the neighborhood for their own profit. And today it is one of the safest and financially stable communities in the city.

The leaders of the religious institutions in that community learned a valuable lesson through their willingness to confront the "principalities and powers." They learned the profound limitations of the church's traditional ministries of presence, prayer, proclamation and practice. Only relational power is sufficient to bring about the change in the systems that in turn brings long-term change to society.

In the final analysis, the ultimate problem is not the people or the churches or the poor themselves. The problem lies with the way the political and economic systems organize to amass and maintain power. And such misuse of unilateral power is, at its root, a spiritual problem.

Therefore, if the problem is not dealt with at its root, it will continue to grow in its exploitation of the people, no matter what the community might do. To simply minister at the level of providing services, advocating for change, preaching the gospel or working to make changes in the community rather than in the systems is to be addressing the *symptom* rather than the true *cause* of the problem. Any such effort will not bring about a permanent resolution of the system's oppression and exploitation of the people. Only organizing the people to amass and use their relational power to confront and hold accountable the systems will bring about substantive change.

There is a postscript to this redlining story. Several weeks after the confrontation of the bank president, the churches and their community organization held a public accountability meeting. Thousands from the churches and neighborhood attended. The community organization announced the agreement with the bank. Selected church, business and neighborhood leaders spoke to the wisdom of the agreement. And then, by prior agreement, the bank president was called upon to respond.

He rose magnificently to the occasion. The president talked about how the bank had been reminded of its community responsibilities by the churches. So the bank had decided to embrace this new partnership with the community and join with the churches in working for its restoration. The thousands at the meeting rose to their feet, cheering the president.

The result of that accountability meeting was that the bank president no longer remained a reluctant participant in this process. Rather, he embraced the new role he had declared for himself in that public meeting and became one of the most enthusiastic, hard-working and influential leaders committed to the rebirth of that community. In a profound sense, that president had acted his way into a new way of thinking.[7] And that bank president had been transformed through the willingness of a large number of people and their institutions to act powerfully.

I hope in my telling of this story that you have gotten the picture of how people power can work to change the intent and directions of systems. But I also hope you noticed the apparent contradiction between this story and what I presented earlier about the nature of unilateral and relational power.

Unilateral power is most used by the institutions of the political, economic and values-building systems, and it seeks to dominate, intimidate and control. Relational power is most exercised by people and people's institutions (churches, community groups, unions, schools), and it seeks to be mutual and reciprocal in its effect. When we were in the bank president's office and presented him with the alternative of either agreeing to our demand or seriously jeopardizing the future of his bank, we weren't acting relationally. We were using the tactics of unilateral power.

But why were we using the tactics of unilateral power? It was not to close down that bank, but to begin a relationship. We did not want the bank to go out of business. We wanted it to do what we believe God's intent is for a neighborhood bank—that is, not only to make a reasonable profit for its investors, but to serve its customers and to redistribute money in the community through loans and other financial services. So our confrontation was meant to make the bank president realize what he was doing and to change his ways. What we really wanted was to build a working relationship with that president and that bank, so we provided through the public accountability meeting the means for him to save face and for us to build a cooperative working relationship with him.

The first step we wanted was public accountability by that bank and its president. We got it! But for Christians, there is something more. We wanted conversion. We hoped to convince our adversary to embrace the God-intended purpose for the bank and for his own life both as an individual and as an institutional leader. And in both, we were successful.

What was Jesus teaching in that hard saying we considered earlier: "Do you think I have come to bring peace to the earth? No, I tell you, but rather division" (Lk 12:51)? He was simply saying that the shalom of society comes only through facing its problems powerfully and the political, economic and value systems creating those problems. Shalom comes about only by confronting even the most powerful troublemakers and being willing to use *power* to require their change. Shalom never occurs by avoiding the problems.

The future of the church lies in our capacity to move out of the comfortable ways we have learned to be "church" in order to embrace church as that community which is in mission to the world. We exist, like Jesus, "to bring good news to the poor, . . . to proclaim release to the captives and recovery of sight to the blind, to let the oppressed go free" and to work for the coming of God's kingdom (Lk 4:18-19). It is only by using the power of relationships that the church can work for the shalom of the city and thus become in deeds, as well as in words, the people of God.

5

NEHEMIAH AND THE
IRON RULE OF POWER

I WAS WORKING IN MY STUDY one afternoon in my inner-city church when there was a knock on my door. When I answered it, I found twenty elderly women who lived in our neighborhood wanting to speak with me. So I ushered them into my study and asked, "How can I help you ladies?"

"Pastor Bob," their spokeswoman, Vivian, said, "we have lived most of our lives here. Some of us were raised in this neighborhood. Others of us moved into it as newlyweds. But all of us have lived our whole adult lives here. This was a wonderful community for raising children. We saw our kids grow up, graduate from high school; many of them got married in our churches. We brought our grandchildren here to be baptized. And some of us have buried our husbands here. All our lives are bound up with this community."

I nodded sympathetically. But Vivian pressed on. "But now our community is being taken away from us. We are afraid of our own community—this neighborhood where we have lived most of our lives."

"How's that?" I asked.

"Crime!" The answer came swiftly, even bitingly. "Crime. We just made a horrible discovery as we were having tea together. We found out that every one of us twenty ladies has been the victim of crime in the past six months.

Some of us have had our purses snatched, some of us have been accosted, some of us have had our homes broken into, one of us was robbed at knifepoint in her very own home. The crime and purse snatching and prostitution and harassment has gotten so bad we're afraid to go out on the streets. Pastor Bob, what are you going to do about it?"

What was I going to do about it? I didn't know what I could do about the crime, prostitution and decay of this community. But there they stood—twenty very determined women. And I had to come up with a response. I began thinking fast!

"Ladies," I replied, "I don't know what to do about crime in this neighborhood. But I know someone who does—our community organizer. Let's go to him and you can tell him the story you just told me."

They agreed. So I called the organizer, Bob, and warned him that twenty angry women and I were coming over to see him. He met us at the door and ushered us into the meeting room of our neighborhood organization. Bob asked an entirely different question than I had asked: "What's your problem?"

"What's our problem? I'll tell you our problem," Vivian replied. And then she began her recital of these women's concern all over again. I waited in breathless anticipation for the punch line to come. And come it did!

"Mr. Bob, what are you going to do about it?"

The organizer's response hit me like a fist. He replied, "I'm not going to do anything about it. It's not my problem. It's your problem. What are *you* going to do about it?"

"What are *we* going to do about it?" Vivian exasperatedly answered. "What can we do about it? We're nothing but little old ladies!"

"You may be little old ladies," Bob responded. "But you are *not* 'nothing but little old ladies'! You are very powerful little old ladies. And if you want to do something to stop crime in this community, you can."

"But we don't know what to do," Vivian answered.

"Of course you don't know what to do," Bob shot back, "because if you had known what to do, you would have already done it, and there wouldn't be the problem of crime that you face now. But that's my job as an organizer, to help you to figure out what to do and to train you to do it. The point is, however, that if you want crime to disappear from this neighborhood, *you have to make it stop yourself.*"

Then Bob drove his message home. "It comes down to a simple choice. Do you really want to stop crime in this neighborhood? Or do you simply want to stand around and complain about how bad it is? Will you or won't you take charge of stopping crime in this neighborhood? That's what I want to know from you."

The ladies looked at each other. And then Vivian answered for them all: "We want to stop it!"

"Okay," responded the organizer. "Let's get to work."

And work they did! And stop it they did. In three months, these "little old ladies" organized hundreds of people in that neighborhood to confront both the chief of police and the mayor and won a significant increase in the number of police patrols, police confrontation of organized crime, and for the first time in over thirty-five years, police *walking* beats in that neighborhood.

What I had seen demonstrated by that organizer was the Iron Rule of organizing—and what ought to be the Iron Rule of all ministries: *Never do for others what they can do for themselves.* That Iron Rule was profoundly expressed in an understanding of ministry not as helping and serving people, but as enabling people to help themselves.

NEHEMIAH AND THE EMPOWERMENT OF ISRAEL

The biblical person who most clearly understood the Iron Rule was Nehemiah. His story is a powerful story of how godly people can use power to transform the life of a city and a nation. The book of Nehemiah illustrates how to use relational power to bring about social transformation.

Who was Nehemiah? The text tells us that he was "cupbearer to the king" of Persia (Neh 1:11). Those few simple words belie his actual position. Nehemiah was one of the highest government officials in the largest empire of its time—an empire that had its origins in present-day Iran but, in Nehemiah's time, stretched from the western border of India through the Turkish peninsula to the Mediterranean Sea, from the Caspian and Black seas to the border of Egypt. As cupbearer, Nehemiah was the personal servant of the Persian emperor Artaxerxes. He tested and served the great king his wine each day, met daily with the king regarding affairs of state and played the role of prime minister of the Persian empire. He was well rewarded for this service, having both great wealth and great influence in the empire.

Nehemiah begins his story with these words:

> In the month of Chislev, in the twentieth year [of Artaxerxes], while I was in
> Susa the capital, one of my brothers, Hanani, came with certain men from
> Judah; and I asked them about the Jews that survived, those who had escaped
> the captivity, and about Jerusalem. They replied, "The survivors there in the
> province who escaped captivity are in great trouble and shame; the wall of
> Jerusalem is broken down, and its gates have been destroyed by fire." When
> I heard these words I sat down and wept and mourned for days, fasting and
> praying before the God of heaven. (Neh 1:1-4)

Begin by building relationships. The first step Nehemiah took to empower Israel in this time of great vulnerability and apparent helplessness
was to build relationships. And he did this by asking questions and listening. He began by asking his brother and "certain men from Judah," in
essence, "How is it going with the Jews that survived the Babylonian captivity, and how is it in Jerusalem?" What Nehemiah heard, in response,
was an earful.

When the great Persian king Cyrus conquered the Babylonian empire in
539 B.C., he reversed the Babylonian policy regarding political captives. To
maintain control over conquered nations, Babylonia brought to its capital
city the political, economic and religious leadership of each nation it conquered, including Israel. When Cyrus overthrew the Babylonian empire, he
allowed the captive elite to return to their countries on the condition that
they would function under the authority of the Persian crown. A significant
number of Israelite captives thus returned home to Judah and its capital city,
Jerusalem. Nehemiah was asking about the descendants of these captives, as
well as those who remained behind in Jerusalem.

As he talked with Hanani and many others, the grave situation facing Israel clearly emerged. Both the Jewish leaders and the people were in profound despair. Those in Babylonian exile had returned to see that Jerusalem
was only a shadow of its former self. It was a razed city, with the people making do as best they could among its ruins. The city's walls were broken
down, leaving its citizens vulnerable to the lightning raids of tribal peoples
who would come sweeping in from the Arabian desert to loot, pillage and
rape. The economy was in shambles, there was no temple to centralize worship, and the Gentile political authorities were economically exploiting the

people. Worst of all, the Jews living in Palestine had lost much of their cultural identity: many no longer spoke Hebrew, temple worship and liturgical rituals were no longer being observed, and the Israelites had lost most of their cultural and religious distinctives. The result was a nation in a vast, corporate depression; all that had made them uniquely Jewish had been taken from them, and they felt helpless and hopeless.

Nehemiah does something significant about all this bad news. He simply keeps asking questions, probing and listening to the stories people have to tell. But he doesn't seem to do anything other than ask questions and listen.

Nehemiah understood that if you want a people to take charge of their own situation and to solve their own problems, the way to do that is not for you to determine the solution to their problems and implement it. All that will do is create dependency on the part of the people. The way you get them to do it for themselves is to get them to share their problems publicly so that they will get angry enough to do something about them. And how you get them to articulate these problems is to ask questions and listen to their responses. But that's not all.

Internalize the pain. The text tells us that Nehemiah also "sat down and wept, and mourned for days" (Neh 1:4). Nehemiah allowed his heart to be broken by the things that were breaking the hearts of his people.

It is not enough for the organizer, community worker or pastor to listen and learn from the people. In order to build the depth of relationships on which relational power is based, you must allow the people's pain to become your pain. And that means allowing the anger and frustration of the people to connect with your anger.

The Latin root for anger is the word *grief*. Authentic anger is the process of grieving over the injustice our people are facing, and connecting that injustice with the pain we have experienced in our own lives. All of us have experienced injustice when we were dominated, oppressed or exploited in ways that diminished our sense of self-worth and self-respect. Those incidents may be overwhelming (such as Israel's oppression under Egyptian slavery) or may seem trivial to someone else (like being made to clean up someone else's mess at summer camp), but they are still injustices to us that made us feel less than human. Our response may have been rage or tears or frustration or grief, but all of these are simply manifestations of anger.

Organizers differentiate between "hot anger" and "cold anger." Hot anger is the immediate response of anger one feels to an unjust situation—it is literally a flush of heat. If you respond to that flush of hot anger, your response will tend to be immediate, visceral and not thought through. Therefore it will likely be destructive.

Cold anger, on the other hand, is anger that is allowed to ferment inside of us as we examine the injustice in a cognitive, reasoned way. In that greater reflection, we will decide if it is in our best interest to respond to that injustice, and if so, what would be the most productive way of responding. When we say after we have responded out of hot anger, "I wish I would have said . . ." we are actually saying, "I wish I had allowed my anger to cool down so I could have spoken in a way that would have gotten the results I wanted.'"

When Nehemiah first heard of the plight of his fellow Jews thousands of miles away in Jerusalem, he likely felt hot anger. But he gave himself time to reflect on it while continuing to talk to other Jews coming to Susa, so that gradually the problem shifted from being the Jews' problem to becoming Nehemiah's problem, as well.

Pray for the people. The text tells us that Nehemiah "fast[ed] and pray[ed] before the God of heaven," and then it presents a sample of his prayers (Neh 1:4-11). Prayer was a strategic part of the process by which Nehemiah prepared both himself and the Jewish people for the great work of liberation God would do through them.

It is instructive to examine Nehemiah's model prayer for insights about how to pray when building relational power (Neh 1:5-11). First, the opening of Nehemiah's prayer is a *prayer of intercession,* simply bringing the plight of the people before God over and over again. Did God need to be convinced that his people were in trouble? Hardly! God was well aware of "the trouble we are in" (Neh 2:17). But God wanted *Nehemiah* to be deeply sensitive to that trouble and to incarnate it into the very pores of his being. Thus prayer is often for the purpose of agitating us, awakening within us the pain of the injustice others, or we, are facing so that we are willing to work for change.

Second, Nehemiah offers to God *prayers of confession.* Note that he includes himself and his family in that confession: "Hear the prayer of your servant that I now pray . . . for your servants, the people of Israel, confessing the sins of the people of Israel, which we have sinned against you. *Both I and my family have sinned"* (1:6, emphasis mine). Nehemiah doesn't try to white-wash the culpability of Israel in contributing to their sorry state. Rather he is very open that "we have offended you deeply, failing to keep the com-mandments, the statutes, and the ordinances that you commanded your ser-vant Moses" (Neh 1:7). As God leads Nehemiah in his prayers to include himself as part of the problem, Nehemiah comes to identify with his people's injustice and pain—and even their sin. This enables him to lead his people and thus carry out an incarnational ministry among them.

Third, Nehemiah prays *prayers of identification*. Through his prayers Ne-hemiah is coming to perceive the depth of the task that lies before him in building a people of power (Neh 1:9). The problem the Israelites have iden-tified as their primary issue is their broken-down walls. That is their most immediate problem, and that is where Nehemiah will organize them to take their first actions. But in this prayer Nehemiah realizes that the essential problem of Israel is far greater than broken-down walls. It is their broken-down corporate life. They no longer know what it means to be Jews. They have lost their cultural and spiritual identity, and until they reclaim that identity, they can never become what they were created by God to be—builders of the shalom community.

Finally, Nehemiah prays *prayers of supplication* (Neh 1:10-11). He asks God to give to him and to the Jews clarity about what they need to do as they act in "cold anger" to rebuild walls and their common life—and even to take the next immediate steps that must be taken to convince a king to cooperate with the will of the people.

Consider your resources. Nehemiah 1 ends with a peculiar sentence: "At the time, I was cupbearer to the king" (Neh 1:11). Why is this sentence here? It is there simply because, besides listening to the people, allowing their pain to become his pain, praying for them and building relational power together with them, Nehemiah reflects on the resources he and Israel could bring to deal with the problems. He does not yet have the trust or commitment of the people. He does not yet have access to the material resources he needs if the people are to rebuild the walls. He does not yet have the permission of the king. But he does have one thing: he is cupbearer to the king. And how he uses that office will determine whether or not he will be able to organize the people of Israel to rebuild their city and their life together.

Understand the value of timing. Perhaps one of the most important traits in Nehemiah's leadership was his consummate sense of timing. The text tells us Nehemiah first became aware of the terrible situation in Israel "in the month of Chislev in the twentieth year [of Artaxerxes]" (Neh 1:1). It further tells us that Nehemiah took his first step of action "in the month of Nisan in the twentieth year" (Neh 2:1). So the period between the months of Chislev and Nisan was the period of incubation—of meeting with the people, listening to their stories, reflecting on their pain, praying over the situation, considering the available resources and building the relationships. And it was not until the month of Nisan that Nehemiah finally acted.

How long was this period of preparation? It took Nehemiah about *six months* to do the silent work "behind the scenes"—the slow, steady work of building relationships—before he had built sufficient power to act.

Martin Buber, the famed Jewish mystic of the early twentieth century, once wrote, "When a man grows aware of a new way in which to serve God, he should carry it with him secretly, and without uttering it, for nine months, as though he were pregnant with it, and let others know of it only at the end of that time, as though it were a birth."[1] Buber reminds us that if we are to be led by God, we must allow time for God to do work in us. A new insight must be given time to incubate. The pain of a people must be given the opportunity to grow within us. Relationships must be carefully nurtured. We must not be so caught up in obtaining results that we do not give God the opportunity to do the greater work that must be done in us if truly systemic change is to take place in our society.

Build first actions on relationships. Finally it is time for Nehemiah to act. The first actions are those of getting the permission of the king and accessing the resources he needs. To accomplish these steps, Nehemiah is going to depend on the relationships he has built over the years.

First, he meets with King Artaxerxes and makes several requests of him (Neh 2:1-8). He asks (1) that he be permitted to go to Jerusalem to investigate and assess the situation; (2) if the situation is as the people have reported, that he be authorized to organize the people to rebuild their walls; (3) that the king guarantee safe passage for Nehemiah to Jerusalem; (4) that the king be willing to have the Persian empire supply the materials (timber, rocks, and so on) at no charge, if Nehemiah decides the walls need to be rebuilt; (5) that the king write personal letters to the appropriate government officials authorizing Nehemiah's requests of them. The king agrees to all of these.

Second, Nehemiah meets with the queen to inform her of his plans (Neh 2:6). This is likely done to guarantee that the king will not renege on any of the agreements. Third, Nehemiah begins his journey to Jerusalem but diverts from that journey to visit with the "governors of the province beyond the river" and with Asaph, keeper of the king's forest, in order to get their cooperation (Neh 2:8-9). Finally, Nehemiah may have met with Sanballat, the governor of the Persian province in which Judea and Jerusalem lay, and with Tobiah the Ammonite official, the most wealthy person in that province and a colleague of Sanballat (Neh 2:10).[2]

We see Nehemiah doing two things in terms of empowerment. First, he is *initiating action on the organizing effort* by getting agreements from the appropriate government officials. He builds that action upon previous relationships that provide him with credibility. Thus his first approach is to negotiate with them and to seek their cooperation based on his relationship with the king. This approach works with the queen, governors and Asaph; it fails with Sanballat and Tobiah.

Second, Nehemiah is *conducting a power analysis.* He is determining the relative power of each of the key government and business leaders with whom he will have to deal if the walls of Jerusalem are to be rebuilt. He needs to know each person's sphere of power, his relative strength vis-à-vis the others and his influence on others in power. From his actions later, it is clear that Nehemiah decides that Sanballat and Tobiah, although opposed to the organizing Nehemiah will be doing, are relatively isolated and are not key players in the Persian power structure. Therefore he determines he can confront them with impunity if they don't cooperate (and they don't).

Assess the situation yourself. Nehemiah arrives in Jerusalem. Thus far he has built strong relationships with those Israelites who had visited him in Susa. He has evaluated the resources available, has undertaken initial actions with the king and others based on his credibility and relationships with them, and has conducted a power analysis. Now he has to build further relationships with the people of Jerusalem and assess the situation himself (as he promised the king he would do). Nehemiah 2:11-16 is the record of the personal research he conducted. As a result of doing so, he concludes that everything he has been told by the Jews in his meetings with them is indeed true. It is therefore time to act.

Publicly identify with the people. Nehemiah calls a great public meeting. To that meeting he invites the Jews (the ordinary Jewish men), the priests (the religious system), the nobles (the political system), the officials (the economic system) and "the rest" (the Jewish women and children, servants, slaves and so on) (Neh 2:16). He climbs onto a platform so that all can see and hear him and makes one of the most compelling speeches in Israel's history.

> Then I said to them, "You see the trouble we are in, how Jerusalem lies in ruins with its gates burned. Come, let us rebuild the wall of Jerusalem, so that we may no longer suffer disgrace." I told them that the hand of my God had been gracious upon me, and also the words that the king had spoken to me. Then they said, "Let us start building!" So they committed themselves to the common good. (Neh 2:17-18)

Virtually every sentence of this remarkable speech is packed with meaning. But the first thing we need to note is that Nehemiah gathers everyone in Israel to listen to it. No one is excluded. Noble and commoner alike, female and male, adult and child, business owner and worker, priest and peasant— all are invited to participate in this action. This is a clear signal that the rebuilding of the walls and corporate life of Israel is going to be a *people's action, not an action of the elite.* The work is not going to be done *for* the people but *by* the people, who must assume its ownership if it is going to succeed.

Second, note how Nehemiah opens his speech: "You see the trouble *we* are in." He begins by identifying himself with the people. He includes himself in their deepest concerns. And that inclusion isn't lost on the crowd.

Publicly articulate the problem. Nehemiah now publicly states the problem in the presence of all the people: "Jerusalem lies in ruins with its gates burned" (Neh 2:17). By publicly declaring the problem, Nehemiah is taking several strategic steps in organizing the people to act powerfully about their situation.

First, by stating the problem, he is making that problem the *immediate* concern with which they need to deal. Nehemiah knew that the primary problem facing Israel was not their broken-down walls but their loss of spiritual and cultural identity. Until they reclaimed the shalom community of Deuteronomy, they would never know peace and well-being as a nation, no matter how tall their walls![3] The vulnerability the Israelites so desperately felt, they had attributed to their broken-down walls. But that vulnerability was actually a manifestation of their deepest problem—a profound spiritual problem.

However, *the people didn't discern that.* Only Nehemiah did. But Nehemiah didn't try to force his insight on them. He knew what they were concerned about, because he had talked with so many of them. So, like any good organizer, Nehemiah began where the people were—organizing around their *perceived* issues and biding his time until, through the continuing process of *action and reflection,* the people would themselves come to the conclusion that their problem was a spiritual one (which they did; see Neh 8—9). And once they perceived their problem as spiritual, they undertook solutions far more radical than Nehemiah would have recommended.

But can the strategy Nehemiah used in a relatively settled and static Jewish community work in today's urban setting? After all, if there is one thing we can depend on today, it is that any neighborhood's people and problems keep changing. Transience, chaos, instability, fear and intimidation, crime and gangs, and lack of consensus are all hallmarks of our cities. But today's successful organizing efforts in the 133 largest cities in the United States, as well as around the world, demonstrate that even in the most transient and chaotic neighborhoods people can be brought together around their issues and, through an ongoing process of action and reflection, empower themselves to solve those issues and transform their communities.[4]

Second, by publicly articulating the problem, Nehemiah gains public ownership of it and thus makes it possible for the people to do something about it. Most people keep a problem to themselves and think they are the only person facing it. Consequently they blame themselves for having the problem. When the problem is articulated publicly and they perceive that many are having the same problem, they begin to feel support, stop blaming themselves and begin to work with others to solve the problem.

For example, a single mother may be having trouble with her son in school. No matter what she does, her son seems to be falling further and further behind in his schoolwork. She begins to think her son is not very bright and that she is a rotten parent. She has had private conferences with the teacher and the school counselor, who suggest all sorts of things she could do to improve her son's learning capacity (some of which she can't afford).

With everything they say, the conviction is reinforced that she is a rotten parent and that her son is not very bright.

But then she visits with another parent in the community who says she is also having trouble with her children in the same school. That parent invites her to a meeting of other parents, and in that larger meeting she hears many parents share how poorly their children are doing and how the school keeps suggesting courses of action that are financially unfeasible for any of the parents to implement. Suddenly the problem changes. Not all these children can be that stupid! Not all these parents could be so bad! Perhaps the problem lies not so much with these parents and children but with the school and the resources they are *not* making available to these children. By publicly articulating the problem, it has moved from being private to public and from blaming self to blaming the shortfall of the educational system. That was what Nehemiah accomplished by publicly talking about the broken-down walls.

Turning the problem into an issue. "Come, let us rebuild the wall of Jerusalem, so that we may no longer suffer disgrace" (Neh 2:17). At first glance it appears that Nehemiah is turning the problem into a solution (that is, the problem is broken-down walls; the solution is to rebuild the walls). But that is not what he is doing at all. Rather he is turning the problem into an issue.

A problem is a complex situation that, because of its size and complexity, is so amorphous that it is difficult to determine a simple plan of resolution. Thus the problem facing Israel ("Jerusalem lies in ruins with its gates burned"), while appearing simple, is really quite complex. What do you need to do to reverse Jerusalem lying in ruins?

Obviously, the walls need to be rebuilt. But so do the streets and the homes and the temple. The market square needs to be reopened and business needs to be able to be conducted there. Provision needs to be made for handling traffic, providing drinking water to the populace and removing body waste and trash. And a palace needs to be built for the governor. The problem of rebuilding Jerusalem is a complex, amorphous situation.

The old African proverb asks, "How do you eat an elephant?" One bite at a time! The purpose of an issue is to reduce the problem to bite size. Remove all the possible tasks that are capturing your attention and select a single task to do. Then it requires a response—"Will you or won't you undertake this action?"

This is what Nehemiah was doing. He was, in essence, asking them, "Will you or won't you rebuild the wall?" For the time being, forget about the streets, the houses, the public buildings, the temple, water access, waste removal. Will you or won't you rebuild the walls? There are only two ways to answer that challenge. Either the people will do it, or they won't.

The people determine the issue. Until this point, Nehemiah is playing the pivotal role as organizer of the people. Now the role radically changes as the people assume the full ownership and leadership of the organizing process: "Then they said, 'Let us start building!' So they committed themselves to the common good" (Neh 2:18). The people decide they are going to organize themselves to rebuild the walls of Jerusalem. Nehemiah isn't going to do it. The Persian government isn't going to do it (Neh 2:1-8). The people will take charge of their own situation and solve their own problem. They take on that issue and rebuild the walls.

The people create their own strategy. Chapter three lays out the plans for the rebuilding of the walls. The strategy was to assign each extended Jewish family (usually fifteen to fifty people) the task of rebuilding a designated portion of the wall. The strategy was that each family would build in concert with the families to its right and left, so that the entire wall would be raised evenly over its entirety. This would provide significant stability to the growing wall.

It is particularly significant that, whenever possible, families were assigned to build in front of their houses (Neh 3:28-29). Thus those creating the building plan intentionally used the self-interest of the people to accomplish the building: they would build their portion of the wall very securely because it was guarding access to their home.

However, the most important reality about this plan of action is found in what *does not* appear in the text. There is no mention of Nehemiah having anything to do with the formation of the strategy. The *people* developed it as they implemented their commitment to rebuild.

The people carry out the action. The book of Nehemiah now moves to a report on the people's implementation of their strategy (Neh 3—5). How they carried out that action plan is significant. They began by having the high priest Eliashib lead his fellow priests in rebuilding the Sheep Gate (Neh 3:1). When they completed the gate, its towers, beams and doors, the entire community gathered to dedicate it. After the dedication all the families set to work to rebuild the wall.

The strategy used here is particularly empowering. Before beginning "this great work," those organizing the rebuilding had the most highly respected people in the nation construct the symbolic entrance to the city and then dedicated it. They were communicating to the people that all Jews—from the least to the greatest—were involved. Such manual labor was beneath no one! And by dedicating the gate, they celebrated their first small accomplishment. By celebrating small victories along the way, and not simply at the completion of the walls, they kept up hope and spirits. One small accomplishment, celebrated at the beginning, infuses confidence, encourages others to get involved and creates the conviction that the action can be accomplished.[5]

The people confront and defeat the systems. The success of the Israelites in their effort to rebuild the walls created opposition by the political system (symbolized by Sanballat, the governor of Palestine), the economic system (symbolized by Tobiah, the Ammonite official) and those people who were not Jews (who were intimidated by the renewed energy of Israel). That opposition took three forms. First, the political and economic systems and the non-Jewish people mocked the efforts of the Jews, making light of their accomplishment. Second, when that didn't work, they threatened Israel with violence. Third, when that reaction failed, these opposing systems and people groups attempted a coup to overthrow Nehemiah (Neh 4:1-5, 7-14; 6:1-9).

Note how Nehemiah and the Jews responded to these three attempts by outside interests to block their rebuilding effort. When mocked, the Israelites simply ignored the taunts; they didn't take the mockery seriously and just went right on building (Neh 4:6). When threatened with violence, however, the Israelites took that threat quite seriously. They divided the Hebrew workforce in half, with one group doing the construction for a period of time and the other standing guard; then at a prearranged time they traded roles (Neh 4:15-23). As they worked, the builders kept their swords with them so that both groups were armed for battle. It is not clear whether it was Nehemiah or the leaders of the people who devised this plan of action, but it is made clear that Nehemiah worked alongside the others in constructing the wall and did not take off his own sword for the duration (Neh 4:23).

The third attempt by Sanballat, Tobiah and the Gentiles to block the rebuilding effort was to entrap Nehemiah in an attempted coup. The coup leaders sought to lure him by asking him to attend a negotiating session with Sanballat; the objective was to capture him while he sat "at the table" and to assassinate him. Whereas negotiation is an integral strategy of any organizing effort, Nehemiah sensed that the invitation to negotiate was a ruse to eliminate him. So he twice refused to attend (Neh 6:1-9, 10-13). Intriguingly, when Sanballat threatened to report Nehemiah's action to Artaxerxes (interpreting his actions as an effort to rebel against Persia), in essence Nehemiah replied, "Go right ahead! Report me to the king. See what trouble it will get you into" (Neh 6:6-9). Nehemiah was confident in the trust relationship he had spent years building with Artaxerxes. He need not fear any such threat.

Here we see demonstrated both Nehemiah's clear understanding of how power was being wielded in this situation and a determination of the appropriate strategy to act in the most powerful way possible that would enable him to accomplish the aim of rebuilding the wall. Good organizers or leaders have to be "wise as serpents and innocent as doves" (Mt 10:16).

Nehemiah confronts the principalities and powers of Israel. It would be expected that "outside" systems and people would oppose the rebuilding of Jerusalem's walls. What came as a particularly bitter pill for Nehemiah to swallow, however, was betrayal by his own countrymen. A number of the Jews working on the wall came to Nehemiah with "a great outcry." They reported that a number of wealthy and powerful Jewish leaders were taking advantage of the circumstances created by the rebuilding of the walls to make significant money and to gain power at the people's expense (Neh 5:1-5).

Because the people were rebuilding the walls, they could not work their fields enough to generate adequate income. Therefore they had to turn to rich Jewish leaders for short-term loans. Those leaders were requiring the people to commit their fields, vineyards, houses and even children as collateral for those loans, and they charged exorbitant interest, though both collateral and interest were forbidden by the Deuteronomic code. The leaders were now foreclosing on those loans, taking away the people's birthright and even taking their sons and daughters as payment—turning the sons into slaves and the daughters into prostitutes. "We are powerless," the people complained to Nehemiah, "and our fields and vineyards now belong to others" (Neh 5:5).

Note what Nehemiah does when he learns of this injustice occurring "inside the camp." He begins by telling us, "I was very angry when I heard their outcry and their complaints. After thinking it over, ..." (Neh 5:6). Nehemiah's first reaction is to be angry; he experiences "hot anger"! But then he thinks it over. Intriguingly the Hebrew phrase translated "After thinking it over . . ." actually says, "But I took counsel with myself." He sat down and had a conversation with himself about what he should do. In other words, he changed his anger from "hot anger" to "cold anger" and calmly and calculatedly developed the following plan of action.

First, Nehemiah meets with "the nobles and the officials" (the Jewish political and economic elite) who are making profit off the financial straits of their brother and sister Jews (Neh 5:7). He confronts them privately about what they were doing, making it clear to them that they were breaking the law. They are "put on notice" that they are going to be held accountable for their actions.

Second, Nehemiah calls "a great assembly" of all the people (Neh 5:7-13). At the assembly, Nehemiah places the economic and political leaders on trial, literally facing their accusers—the people. He has the people tell their stories of the exploitation and oppression they and their children are experiencing from these leaders. Nehemiah then confronts the leaders, summarizing the crime of which they are accused: breaking the Deuteronomic law (Neh 5:8). He then presents the people's demand to the leaders: "The thing that you are doing is not good. . . . Let us stop this taking of interest. Restore to them, this very day, their fields, their vineyards, their olive orchards, and their houses, and the interest on money, grain, wine, and oil that you have been exacting from them" (Neh 5:9-11).

The Jewish political and economic leaders, overwhelmed at such public confrontation, reply, "We will restore everything and demand nothing more from them. We will do as you say." But Nehemiah won't accept their verbal agreement. He makes them sign a legally binding contract by having them take an oath before the Israelite priests and the people (Neh 5:12). He then concludes by declaring that they will be banned from Israel if they do not conform to this agreement. The assembly supports him in these demands. And the confrontation ends with the word, "And the people [that is, the political and economic leaders] did as they had promised" (Neh 5:13).

The people celebrate their victory.

> So the wall was finished on the twenty-fifth day of the month Elul, in fifty-two days. And when all our enemies heard of it, all the nations around us were afraid and fell greatly in their own esteem; for they perceived that this work had been accomplished with the help of our God. (Neh 6:15-16)

The wall was now completed. The initial organizing effort of the people was now finished. When Nehemiah first began meeting with the Israelites, he found them dispirited, helpless, marginalized. Now Israel had a sense of pride, self-assurance and power that had come as the result of rebuilding their walls. They not only *could* do it; they *did* do it! And because they had so successfully rebuilt their walls, the nations around them looked upon this newfound pride and, in comparison, "fell greatly in their own esteem." Power had come to the Israelites because they had assumed power.

So the people gathered together to celebrate their great victory, to praise God and to recognize what they had accomplished (Neh 8:1-18). They had rebuilt their wall. Now they were ready to begin to rebuild their life together as children of the covenant and followers of the Deuteronomic law.[6]

LESSONS FROM NEHEMIAH

In his use of relational power, Nehemiah presents an alternative to the pattern of ministry often used by churches or mission agencies today. If a church becomes interested in reaching out beyond itself, the pattern it will most likely adopt will be that of doing ministry *to* the city. That is, it will likely undertake a study of its community in order to gather information. It may conduct an opinion survey, but the church decides what information it will consider and what to do with that information. It is not an objective of the church to build a mutual relationship with the people. Rather the people are essentially treated as objects supplying wanted data for the survey.

With this information gathered from church and community, the church will determine what the primary issue or problem is that it intends to address and will create the program or project it believes will most significantly address that problem. The church or mission agency will then mobilize its resources to implement that program and will run the program for the community so that the people are perceived by the church as clients or recipients of that program. The project may be very comprehensive in nature and will definitely be well intentioned. But it will remain under the control of the church or mission agency and will run by the regulations it has established.

The inevitable result of conducting ministry *to* the city is that there is little or no investment in or commitment to this project or ministry by the people it is meant to serve. They did not create it; they did not determine it should be created; they do not assume responsibility for its operation; and they will have little or nothing to say about its eventual dissolution. The inevitable result is that the project will continue only as long as its sponsoring church or agency is willing to provide the volunteers or staff and the finances and the facilities that make the project function.

The tragedy is that this does not empower the people it is designed to help. Rather it patronizes them by treating them as clients or recipients. By its very nature it treats people as objects in need of help. In turn that erodes the people's confidence in their own abilities and contributes to their lack of self-respect. Ministry *to* the city does not treat people as capable of self-determined action and of assuming responsibility for their own destiny. Treating people as objects deepens their sense of powerlessness. It reinforces their sense of helplessness, making them feel patronized, inadequate and rejected by the larger society.

However, the most profound weakness of this approach to ministry is what it does to the church or mission agency that insists on carrying on ministry *to* the people of the community. When the church seeks to solve people's problems by providing social services to them but doesn't challenge the systemic sources of those problems, it is addressing the symptoms rather than the causes. If it concentrates on addressing those symptoms, the church is abdicating its responsibility to call the systems to accountability (Eph 3:10). When the church refuses to challenge the systemic sources of the problems its services are meant to alleviate, it actually contributes to the maintenance and sustenance of the dominating political, economic and religious systems it is called by God to challenge.

The Nehemiah approach is a radically different way of doing ministry in a community or a larger society. Rather than conducting ministry *to* the city, the Nehemiah approach is one of doing ministry *with* the city. Nehemiah did not conduct a survey of the people. Rather he listened to them, learned from them and built relationships with them. Out of those growing relationships of trust, Nehemiah could then work with the people to identify the issues for themselves (rebuild the walls of Jerusalem) and to create and implement their own strategy to substantively address those issues (including dealing with and, if necessary, confronting the "principalities and powers").[7]

Thus Nehemiah's approach to ministry was to bring together the previously marginalized, powerless people of Israel, so that

- they could analyze the issues
- they could determine their own solutions
- they could implement the actions to carry out those solutions
- they could evaluate the results
- they could celebrate their own victories
- they could move on to tackle the next (and more substantive) issue before them

The approach to ministry being suggested here is one in which a church or mission agency—both its leaders and its people—perceive themselves as being a part of a larger community sharing common hopes, issues and problems that cannot be successfully addressed either by each group doing its own work or by appealing to the largess of the systems. Only organizing together around the common issues of those church members and the people of the community—whether it's broken-down walls or crime or education—and requiring the systems to be responsive will bring about substantive change in that community. And such organizing together cannot happen unless considerable time has been given to building relationships of trust with each other as people share the struggles of their lives, the values they hold in common and the issues that are making life miserable for them. Only by building relational power can the lives of people be changed and their communities socially transformed.

Nehemiah 6:15 tells us that it took fifty-two days to rebuild the walls of Jerusalem—once the people put their mind to "this great work." The reconstruction of those walls and their subsequent dedication was completed by October 2, 445 B.C. But in the midst of the joy of a work well done, it is easy for us to overlook the fact that those walls had been demolished for *141 years!*

For 141 years, the Jewish people had tolerated the demolition of their walls. They had put up with the loss of protection against marching armies, the looting and pillaging by marauding bands, the raping of their wives and daughters, the burning and destruction of their homes and public buildings, the leveling of their temple. For 141 years, they were oppressed by the Babylonians and the Persians and were exploited by local tribes and even their own Jewish elite. They had believed that they were a nation of nobodies, a people marginalized by their religion and by their belief in an apparently dormant God. Because their city's walls were broken down, the Jewish people accepted the abuse of the rest of the world, making them into second-class citizens. Yet, as Nehemiah demonstrated to them, the power to change their situation had lain in their own hands. At any time during those 141 years, they could have chosen to rebuild their walls!

The question that must therefore be asked is this: Why did the Jews not say, sometime during those 141 years, "We're not going to take this anymore"? Why did they take such abuse from the tribes around them, the desert people pillaging them, the nations oppressing them? Why did they choose to remain in such bondage?

The answer is simple. They lacked a Nehemiah. They lacked a person who would ask questions, who would listen to their pain, who would learn from the people, who would build relationships with them, who would allow his heart to be broken with that pain, who would pray to God for them, who would assess the resources at hand, who would not be afraid of stepping out into public life and confronting even an emperor, and who would gather the people and declare to them, "You see the trouble we are in, how

Jerusalem lies in ruins with its gates burned. Come, let us rebuild the wall of Jerusalem!"

But once they found a person who both believed in and carried out in his own ministry the Iron Rule of Power—"Never do for others what they can do for themselves"—well then, dear reader, Israel was reborn!

6

JESUS IS CAESAR
Paul's Theology of Power

NEXT TO JESUS CHRIST, the apostle Paul was the most strategic player
in the formation of Christianity. Paul was profoundly influential in the way
Christianity developed, thought and acted as it spread beyond Israel into
"the uttermost parts" of the Roman Empire.

Paul was the first Christian leader to realize that as long as Christianity
remained a Jewish sect, it would not have much of a future. He led the
church into reaching out to the Gentile world, founded churches throughout Asia Minor, Greece, Macedonia and Rome (and perhaps Spain), wrote
thirteen books of the Bible (and probably other letters that have since been
lost), founded at least thirteen churches and won countless people to faith
in Jesus Christ. But undeniably Paul's greatest contribution to Christianity
was his formation of a theology upon which the church could reach a Gentile world.

Paul's theology was enriched by his knowledge of Jewish law (he was a
former Pharisee trained under Israel's leading theologian), Greek logic (he
was raised in Tarsus, a Greek colony where he studied Greek logic) and Roman jurisprudence (he was a Roman citizen, highly skilled at using Roman
law to benefit the church). He formulated a theology around the Jewish concept of the *hesed* ("steadfast or grace-filled love") of God that resulted in a
theology of divine grace made accessible to all people through the sacrificial

death of Jesus Christ. His theology of the church, built around the model of the synagogue but adapted to Greek and Roman culture, has become the formative model for the nature and mission of the church for more than two thousand years.

However, Paul was not only an outstanding theologian and builder of the Gentile church. He was also very sophisticated in his understanding of and use of power, and that use of power was built upon a highly developed theology of public life. In this chapter we will examine Paul's clearest and most comprehensive statement of the church's role in public life.

THE WORLD OF PAUL THE APOSTLE

To better understand Paul's insights regarding the church's role in public life, one must understand how Jewish and Gentile people in the first century A.D. perceived the world. To Jew and Gentile alike, the world of the physical and the world of the spiritual were closely intertwined. To ancient humanity, what might happen in the heavenlies would profoundly impact what occurred on earth, and what might happen on earth would influence heaven. Thus Jesus would teach his followers to pray to God,

> Your kingdom come.
> Your will be done,
> on earth as it is in heaven (Mt 6:10),

assuming that if God's will is done in heaven, there is high expectation that it will be done on earth. Or again, Paul teaches that it is inevitable that Christ will someday reign over all the affairs of the earth (Phil 2:10-11). Because Christ already reigns with God the Creator in heaven, it is a foregone conclusion that he will reign here as well.

Because Paul believed there was an open door between the spiritual world and physical world, he held that the governance of both worlds was also irretrievably linked. Thus Paul would build his theology of "the principalities and powers" on the premise that what happens in the spirit world has its counterpart on earth. Therefore the principalities and powers are not solely spiritual forces of heaven and of hell at war with each other. Nor are the principalities and powers simply the political, economic and religious systems of human society. The principalities and powers are both spiritual and earthly, with the heavenly or "hellish" dimension of that power providing the spiritual power that would drive the performance and provide the power to any earthly system.[1]

Because spiritual life is replicated on earth, the conflict between systems and between people and their systems is a duplication of that same conflict in the spiritual world. This is what is meant by "spiritual warfare," as graphically described in the book of Revelation. The battles depicted there between heaven and the underworld have their counterpart in the struggles of the seven churches in Asia Minor as they strived to remain true to the gospel and not be conquered by the seductive forces of their Greco-Roman cultures (Rev 2—3).

A sign of this duplication of the warfare between heavenly systems and the forces of good and evil in the cities and nations of the Roman Empire is the language Paul chose to describe the principalities and powers: "[Jesus] is the image of the invisible God, the firstborn of all creation; for in him all things in heaven and on earth were created, things visible and invisible, whether thrones or dominions or rulers or powers" (Col 1:15-16).

First, note in this statement by Paul that he directly says that the "rulers and powers" have their abode both "in heaven and on earth," and are both "visible" (that is, they are human systems with values—structures like the Sanhedrin and the Roman Senate—and are operated by specific flesh-and-blood human beings) and "invisible" (that is, they are spiritual systems operating in "heaven").

Second, note what he chose to call these heavenly/earthly systems. Here is Paul's standard formula for describing this reality: "thrones, dominions, rulers, powers." But what are thrones, dominions, rulers and powers?

- The *throne* is the symbolic institution of power in a state, city, or economic or religious institution. In its most literal sense, a throne is a "seat" (as we refer to the "seat of government") on which the *principality* sits.

- The *dominion* is the sphere of influence or territory ruled by the throne. Thus the dominion of the Roman Empire was the territory of the empire.

- The *ruler* is the specific person who currently occupies the *throne*. The ruler can change; the throne continues in its rule over that dominion. Thus, when a monarch of Great Britain dies, the people cry, "The king [that specific "prince"] is dead; long live the king [the throne or institution of monarchy]."

- The *powers* (also sometimes translated "authorities") are the sanctions or rules that legitimize the current occupant of the *throne* as the *ruler* over that *dominion,* thus granting to that person the privileges, obligations and limitations accorded those occupying the throne.

Through his theology of the rulers and powers, Paul presented a unique and highly creative analysis of the struggle of the first-century church with the political, economic and religious systems of Rome and of the Jewish state. The book that most clearly presents this struggle—and therefore the necessity for the church to engage in public life—is the book of Ephesians.

The occasion for the writing of Ephesians was the approaching martyrdom of Paul.[2] The apostle was in prison, awaiting his inevitable execution. He knew his execution was only the beginning of what would become an empire-wide persecution of the church by Rome, which now saw the church as posing the greatest threat of any institution to its continued dominance of the world. How could the apostle best prepare his beloved Christians and their churches for the holocaust to come?

One would expect Paul to advise the church to go underground, to make itself invisible, to hunker down for the persecution that would be coming. But that is not what Paul recommends in Ephesians. Rather, he advises the church to assertively move out into and witness to the world. The theology of Ephesians centers on the church as God's redeemed people living in a world of spiritual darkness dominated by an evil empire and its Caesar; God's call to that church is to work toward the transformation of that world into the kingdom of God. And that would occur, Paul contends, only if the church is willing to move aggressively into the public life of Rome and be heard.

PAUL'S CALL TO PUBLIC LIFE

The book of Ephesians has two parts. Chapters one through three deal with the theology of the church's engagement in public life. Chapters four through six outline the practice of that theology through the everyday life and work of the church. Both present Paul's clearest message on the Christian use of power to work for the transformation of society with the gospel.

God's call to the church. Why do we, as Christians, exist? As the church, what are we called by God to be and do? Paul begins Ephesians by reminding us that God "has blessed us in Christ with every spiritual blessing" (Eph 1:3), and then proceeds to recount those blessings.

- God "chose us in Christ before the foundation of the world" (Eph 1:4).

- God "destined us for adoption as his children through Jesus Christ" (Eph 1:5).

- God redeemed us "through [Christ's] blood" and forgave us "our trespasses, according to the riches of his grace that he lavished on us" (Eph 1:7-8).

- God has "made known to us the mystery of his will"—that is, what we are called to do as God's adopted and redeemed children (Eph 1:9).

- God has "marked [us] with the seal of the promised Holy Spirit" (Eph 1:13).

At the very beginning of this most formative book, Paul reminds his churches of who they are. They are the people whom God chose, adopted, redeemed, forgave—to whom God revealed his will and gave the Holy Spirit. But why did God do all this for us? We Christians have been thus encountered by God so we can participate in God's "plan for the fullness of time, to gather up all things in him, things in heaven and things on earth" (Eph 1:10).

The phrase "things in heaven and things on earth" is not a rhetorical statement to Paul. This is the term he coined and then used throughout many of his letters to refer to the political, economic and religious institutions of Rome ("things on earth") and their matching principalities and powers in the spiritual realm ("things in heaven").

What Paul presents here is the challenge that the essential mission of the church is to work for the transformation of the world into God's kingdom. In essence he is saying, "The universe is at war—a war between God and the powers of darkness symbolized by Satan. As emissaries of God, the angels are to wage that war against Satan in the heavenlies. And likewise the church is to be engaged in the same warfare with the political, economic and religious systems of Rome. To wage that war is why God chose you, called you, adopted, redeemed and forgave you, and that is why you have been given the power of the Holy Spirit."

This is Paul's theological rationale for the church not to "hunker down" under persecution but to engage fearlessly in public life. We are to be about winning people to Christ, confronting political systems, transforming economic systems and converting religious (or values-creating) systems. Paul is not suggesting that our involvement in public life is optional or tangential to the purpose, work and life of the church. He is declaring that *involvement in public life is what the church is to be about*. The church is to be involved in public life as its essential mission. It exists for the world! And to settle for anything less is to be unfaithful.

This, of course, is an overwhelming task. The church of the first century was so little—and Rome was so large. In that light, Paul bursts into prayer for his beloved Christians throughout the Roman Empire, that they may know the hope to which God has called them and the "immeasurable greatness of his power" (Eph 1:17-19). Paul's prayer is the prayer of a father who is facing his own death—a prayer for his children who without him must now face the powers of Rome, the dangers of betrayal and the undertaking of an apparently impossible task. So he prays that they will be filled with God's power for the awesome task ahead of them—a power that will give them spiritual discernment, the capacity never to lose the awareness of what God has already done for them in Christ, the determination that they must never "take their eyes off the prize" of an empire won to Christ and the conviction that they are a people of power because they belong to the Lord of all power.

Jesus is Caesar. Emboldened by his prayer, Paul then moves into the most astounding statement of this letter—a proclamation that would guarantee that the church would win the enmity of Rome.

> God put this power to work in Christ when he raised him from the dead and seated him at his right hand in the heavenly places, far above all rule and authority and power and dominion, and above every name that is named, not only in this age but also in the age to come. And he has put all things under his feet and has made him the head over all things for the church, which is his body, the fullness of him who fills all in all. (Eph 1:20-23)

Having reminded the church in his prayer that we Christians are people of God's power, Paul elaborates on the power of God that the church can access as it engages Rome. The power of God is such, Paul states, that God raised Jesus from the dead and has crowned him the monarch of heaven and earth, ruling over every government, head of state, constituting powers of that state and all its territories. Of course Paul is clearly referring to the Roman Empire.

To Christians living in the first century this was clearly and unequivocally *an extreme political statement.* Ephesians 1:20-23 would have been read by any Christian—and any Roman—from the standpoint of the cosmology that an action in heaven would make inevitable its eventual occurrence on earth. Therefore they would immediately see that the following is what Paul was actually declaring:

> God has crowned Jesus as the emperor of heaven. God has already seated Jesus upon the throne and has already placed him over all nations and empires ("thrones" or "rule"), all rulers ("principalities" or "authorities"), all governments ("powers"), and all their territories ("dominions"), both in heaven and on earth, both now ("this age") and as God's will is inevitably worked out through all the governments that are to come ("the age to come").

What Paul so boldly proclaimed is that Christ has already been crowned king over all nations, economic orders and civilizations that do now or will eventually exist. Or, in other words, Paul is here declaring that *Jesus is the true Caesar of the entire world—including Rome.* The man in Rome who presently calls himself "Caesar" is an imposter!

Now do you see why the Christians were persecuted? The real offense that the Christians were to Rome was not that they were of another religion, but that they declared that their Lord was the true and authentic ruler (or "Caesar") of the world. They recognized Jesus as their Caesar, rather than Nero. And that made them a threat to the future of the Roman Empire.

But Paul is not done. He continues, "[God] has made [Jesus] the head over all things for the church, which is his body, the fullness of him who fills all in all" (Eph 1:22-23). Here Paul is declaring that the means by which Jesus will become the ruler over all the Romes of the world ("the head over all things") is through God's use of the church. *The church will be the means God will use to win the world to allegiance to Jesus.* Therefore the church is

118

to work to bring to reality in society what has been preordained because it has already been accomplished in heaven. If the church is faithful in fulfilling this assignment, the world will experience "the fullness of him who fills all in all."

Paul declares that the church—this little band of apparently helpless "nobodies"—has been chosen to be God's means for bringing about the submission of Rome to Christ. Such submission will not happen by the church aping the dominating use of power that the Roman systems use to tyrannize the world. Rather it will happen as the church seeks to influence those systems through its practice of justice with love as it engages the systems through its use of relational power. We are called by God to be change agents in the world. But we will be so used by God only to the degree the church actively involves itself in working for justice and transformation in the public arena.

The church as God's ambassadors. Paul then continues his argument in Ephesians 2:1-10. He reminds Christians that we were once corrupted and even controlled by the systems and the values of Rome, Israel and any other nation, belief system or cause. We were ruled by our desires and passions, exploited and used by the systems. Thus we were "by nature children of wrath, like everyone else" (Eph 2:3). Thus Paul reminds us that we have not been chosen by God to be transformers of the world's systems because we are more holy or righteous or intelligent or such strong leaders. Rather, we were as corrupt and as seduced as is everyone else.

But God has acted to free us from the spiritual, psychological and physical control that the political, economic and religious systems have exercised over us in the past. It is God who freed us, not we ourselves. If it had been up to us, we would still be victims—oppressed, exploited or seduced into cooperation by the economic and political powers of our city and nation, controlled in our thinking, our behavior, and our beliefs by those systems that shape the values of our society. We would be just like all the other people, serving our business and government, and mindlessly parroting the convictions taught us that keep the systems in power.

But God freed us from an unthinking acceptance of servitude to our nation's systems in order to follow his call to work for the transformation of the world into God's kingdom. And God did this through Jesus Christ, who could not be seduced by the systems of Israel because he could see through them. So it is that it is through "grace you have been saved through faith [that is, through placing your trust in a king other than Caesar], and this is not your own doing; it is the gift of God" (Eph 2:8).

God has done this so that we might be "what he has made us, created in Christ Jesus for good works, which God prepared beforehand to be our way of life" (Eph 2:10). The church is to be an ambassador of another Caesar, of a different kingdom, of a profoundly different way of life. We, the church, are to work for our new king to bring about the changes that need to occur in our political, economic and religious systems so that they might increasingly become the systems God created them to be. This is to be "our way of life," prepared before our conversion (or even our birth) for us to do.

The church as sharing in reconciliation. Part of the work Christ has done in and between us is to keep on breaking down the walls of hostility that divide people, nations, racial and ethnic groups, religions, and economic systems (Eph 2:11-14). By bringing us all into the kingdom of God from across every race, ethnicity, nation, religion, economic system and people group, Christ has made us into one new humanity. This he has done by abolishing the power of the systems that will always seek to divide us. Christ has created "in himself one new humanity in place of the two [whatever two might divide us—Jew versus Arab, white versus black, socialist versus capitalist, Irish Catholic versus Irish Protestant], thus making peace, [that he] might reconcile both groups to God in one body through the cross, thus putting to death that hostility through it" (Eph 2:15-16).

In other words, all divisions in the human race are false dichotomies. They are mostly divisions built on events in the distant past over which we have no control, and they have built one upon the other—offense upon offense—until those differences have loomed so large they destroy any potential for reconciliation.

My wife and I are friends with a Muslim Palestinian couple whom we have known for many years. Recently we were together and the conversation came around to the division between Palestinians and Israelis. They spoke hotly on the topic because their family had personally experienced the Israelis taking their land and home away from them. "It is tragic," I said, "that the

Holy Land has been torn with strife between Arab and Israeli for thousands of years."

"No, you do not understand," the husband replied, "We Palestinians have never done anything wrong—never, in all those thousands of years! It is always the Israelis who have taken from us. They are 100 percent in the wrong. All of our killing of them is justified and is always in the right."

Incredulous, I responded, "No Palestinian has ever done anything wrong in this conflict?"

"That is right," he said. "Israel is always wrong and is evil. We are always right and everything we do is justified. Therefore we can never be reconciled to them. The only right thing we can do is to drive them totally from our land."

It is in the self-interest of the political, economic and values-sustaining systems and institutions of a nation to maintain that kind of hatred, because such maintenance necessitates that the systems and their leaders stay in power and even increase their authority. The systems will always divide the world into "us" and "them" because that helps keep the systems in power. But when people come to Christ and adopt his kingdom as their own, their allegiance to their nation, ethnic group or "people" should lessen because they have now embraced a kingdom that knows no ethnic or national boundaries: "You are no longer strangers and aliens, but you are citizens with the saints and also members of the household of God, built upon the foundation of the apostles and prophets, with Christ Jesus himself as the cornerstone" (Eph 2:19-20). Therefore, because they have become the only truly liberated people in the world, the church is to work for the reconciliation of the systems into the one body of people standing under the cross. Thus Paul declares this must be an essential part of the public agenda of the church.

It is important to see what Paul is *not* saying here. He is *not* suggesting that there is no place for human diversity. Our cultural distinctives are important because they capture the unique nuances of our ethnic, racial and national identities. Those differences are worthy of celebration—not only by that people whose distinctives they are but also by all peoples. Otherwise why visit any other culture, enjoy ethnic food or share in national celebrations?

Paul is not suggesting the creation of a society that has no cultural diversity. He is not saying that the task of the church is to work for the reconciliation of the systems into the *same* body of people (how boring that would be!). He is saying that the church is to work for the reconciliation of the systems into the *one* body—culturally and ethnically distinct but not seeking to dominate the world with one nation's or culture's political or economic agenda. Paul is saying that all people and nations and cultures recognize their common humanity under Christ and thus discover *who* they are by discovering *whose* they are.

The church as harbingers of a new social reality. Paul now moves to a description of his unique call and the insights that call can bring to the church about its work in the (Roman) world. By looking at his call, Paul is able to present the clearest statement in Ephesians—and in anything he wrote—about the essential function of the church in the real world.

He moves into this topic by reminding his readers of "the mystery of Christ" that he was privileged to have been given before any other believers. That mystery has come to define his ministry and has now come to be largely accepted by the church, Paul declares. But it is that mystery that also makes clear to us the true and primary mission of the church.

The mystery is that "the Gentiles have become fellow heirs, members of the same body, and sharers in the promise in Christ Jesus through the gospel" (Eph 3:6). That is the reason the church is called to be ambassadors of the gospel and is to work for reconciliation. It is to so work because there should be no division between Gentile and Jew or between any other humanly made or systems-encouraged division that leads to an allegiance to a nation, an economy, a values-system, a Caesar greater than our allegiance to God. Paul is therefore seeking to enable the church to embrace a profoundly expanded life and ministry beyond what anyone can believe or even imagine. And Paul expresses that expansive work of the church in this way:

> [I want] to make everyone see what is the plan of the mystery hidden for ages in God who created all things; *so that through the church the wisdom of God in its rich variety might now be made known to the rulers and authorities in the heavenly places.* This was in accordance with the eternal purpose that he has carried out in Christ Jesus our Lord, in whom we have access to God in boldness and confidence through faith in him. (Eph 3:9-12, emphasis mine)

If all Paul was concerned about was seeing individual Gentiles and Jews come to Jesus Christ, he would have written, "through the church the wisdom of God might now be made known to people." But that is not what he wrote. He is saying that the wisdom of God, which humanity has refused to see, is that there is no need in human society for the existence of political, economic, religious, racial or ethnic dichotomies *that divide humanity.* God never intended us to be divided into "us" and "them." But the political, economic and religious systems of every society, every nation and every city need such divisions in order to maintain their domination. So they foster such divisions.

Therefore the primary work of the church is to proclaim to the world's systems a new vision of the world—a world with all its systems living in a shalom community and thus creating together, through the grace of God, the "kingdom of our Lord and of his Christ." Such a kingdom is not a bland kingdom of sameness, but rather is God's reconciled world "in its rich variety"—the creation of a kaleidoscope of cultures and peoples, all united by a common allegiance to the same Lord, the same "Caesar," Jesus Christ.

In other words, Paul is saying the work of the church goes far beyond preaching the gospel, winning souls to Christ, building up or planting congregations, working for social justice, or even hunkering down in order to preserve the church and to stay alive. Paul is declaring that the work of the church is to hold up to the Roman Empire and to any other system an *entirely different vision* for their society—a vision of all of life lived in shalom under the authority of Christ and manifested in that society's pursuit of a politics of justice, an economics of equitable distribution of wealth, the elimination of poverty and a people in relationship with God. And that "mystery" can only be realized if the church will move beyond itself to be engaged in every possible way in public life.

In light of such a stupendous task, Paul prays that they may have the strength to undertake that task, that they will be able to get their heads around such a vision, that they may be centered in Christ when undertaking such an assignment and that Christ's love will empower them for the task (Eph 3:14-19). He then closes the theological section of this profound book with a benediction, dedicating the church to public life (Eph 3:20-21).

IMPLEMENTING PUBLIC LIFE

If the primary work of the church is to call the Roman Empire (and any subsequent political, economic or religious systems) to embrace the "Caesarship" of Christ and to give themselves to his kingdom of justice, equitable distribution of wealth and relationship with God and each other, how does the church actually go about accomplishing this? How should the church work in order to move society toward the shalom community?

In the second half of Ephesians, Paul answers that question. But he answers it in a highly nuanced way that has confused biblical interpreters ever since. He doesn't provide broad principles that can be applied to any society and in any century. After all, that wasn't to whom he was writing. He was writing to the church in the Roman Empire, and therefore he makes suggestions to the church about their engagement in public life that are relevant for life under the Roman Empire. What we need to do is not to follow his instructions literally but to perceive the essential principles lying behind each instruction and let those principles guide us as to how to move out into public life as today's church.

Unity and the division of labor. Paul begins by reminding his readers of the dominant theme in the first section: "There is one body and one Spirit, just as you were called to the one hope of your calling, one Lord, one faith, one baptism, one God and Father of all, who is above all and through all and in all" (Eph 4:4-6). But then Paul moves on to propose a way of being church that is designed to equip and empower the church to effectively undertake its primary responsibility of engagement in public life.

> The gifts [God] gave were that some would be apostles, some prophets, some evangelists, some pastors and teachers, to equip the saints for the work of ministry, for building up the body of Christ, until all of us come to the unity of the faith and of the knowledge of the Son of God, to maturity, to the measure of the full stature of Christ. . . . Speaking the truth in love, we must grow up in every way into him who is the head, into Christ, from whom the whole body, joined and knit together by every ligament with which it is equipped, as each part is working properly, promotes the body's growth in building itself up in love. (Eph 4:11-13, 15-16)

The traditional way Ephesians 4:12 has been translated results in a distortion of Paul's intent.[3] Verse 12 has normally been translated "to equip the saints, to do the work of ministry, to build up the body of Christ." That translation makes Paul seem to say that those occupying the offices of "apostle, prophet, evangelist, pastor and teacher" have three primary responsibilities: to equip Christians, to undertake the work of ministry and to build up the church. But that is not what the Greek says at all. A more accurate translation is given in the New Revised Standard Version: "to equip the saints for the work of ministry, for building up the body of Christ." In other words, Paul taught the Christians of his day that the primary task of the church's apostles, prophets, evangelists, pastors and teachers is to equip Christians so that *those Christians* can undertake the church's work of ministry, and this shared labor will build up the body of Christ. Only by translating this verse this way can sense be made of the subsequent verses of this section (Eph 4:13-16).

What Paul is stating, in light of the total message of Ephesians, is that the task of the ordained clergy is to prepare Christians for public life. Through worship, prayer, study of Scripture, instruction, training and pastoral support, these leaders were to equip Christians to be engaged in Roman society. But the church would only be a transforming influence in Roman society if each Christian was willing to be involved in public life and was engaged in whatever areas of the political, economic and values-formation life of the empire to which he or she had access. The clergy couldn't do it alone. To change the Roman Empire, it would take every Christian living out their Christianity every day in practical and concrete ways.

Living a new life. Paul taught that the first level of involvement in public life would be in the nature of our lifestyle. If people did not see transformation in the ways we engaged others and conducted our own lives, we would not have credibility in our engagement in the political, economic or values-setting arenas. Paul laid out the characteristics of a transformed public life in Ephesians 4:17—5:20. Here are some examples from the long lists he created:

- "Let all of us speak the truth to our neighbors" (Eph 4:25).

- "Thieves must give up stealing; rather let them labor and work honestly with their hands, so as to have something to share with the needy" (Eph 4:28).

- "Let no evil talk come out of your mouths, but only what is useful for building up, as there is need" (Eph 4:29).

- "Put away from you all bitterness and wrath and anger and wrangling and slander, together with all malice, and be kind to one another, tenderhearted, forgiving one another, as God in Christ has forgiven you" (Eph 4:31-32).

- "Fornication and impurity of any kind, or greed, must not even be mentioned among you" (Eph 5:3).

One may wonder, "What do lists of ethical behavior have to do with public life?" But we must remember that most of the Christians who were won to faith under Paul's ministry had no idea how a Christian should act either in public or in private. They had come from a rather ruthless society that seemed to operate with the code "Do unto others before they do to you." Thus the place to begin training people in public conduct was to present them with a different ethical and moral model.

Marriage, family and work. Paul next presents three arenas of public life in which Christians should be particularly involved, whether they are of high or of low estate: building strong and committed marriages, creating secure and loving families, and conducting just employment practices (Eph 5:21-33; 6:1-4, 5-9). He develops the Christian response in these three institutions by teaching mutual submission—a mutual yielding to each other as opposed to the domination of the powerful (husbands, parents, employers) over the powerless (wives, children, slaves).

Personal lifestyle, marriage, parenting and employment are not often thought of as arenas of public life. But in the Roman Empire these were in fact the primary arenas in which public life could be practiced. Neither the ordinary Roman citizen nor the free peasant was permitted to engage in the political arena; that was reserved exclusively for nobility. Nor could a citizen or free peasant be engaged in the setting of economic policy for the empire or even its free cities; that was reserved for large landowners and people of means (who were most often nobility). Engagement in public life was in the everyday activities at the marketplace, the shop, the public bath, the sports arena, the schools and the homes. But Paul recognized that even given the limitations of involvement in public life in the first-century Roman Empire, if the church was not engaged in the struggles, the insistence on rights, and the defense of the poor and the powerless (even women, children, slaves and workers), its faith would make no difference in the world in which the vast majority of people lived.

The church of God goes forth to war. Ephesians ends with the striking metaphor of the church as a Roman soldier clad in defensive armament (belt of truth, breastplate of righteousness, shoes of the gospel of peace, shield of faith, helmet of salvation) and with weapons of offense (sword of the Spirit) ready to do battle in the public arena. "For our struggle is not against enemies of blood and flesh," Paul states, "but against the rulers, against the authorities, against the cosmic powers of this present darkness, against the spiritual forces of evil in the heavenly places" (Eph 6:12).

Returning to the theme with which he began the book, Paul reminds the reader that when the Christians engage in public life, they are in "spiritual warfare," for they must battle the manifestations of spiritual principalities and powers that possess the political, economic and values-sustaining systems of Rome, Israel and all other societies. It is a struggle to the death, and the church has not carried out its calling from God if all it seeks to do is to win souls, plant congregations and build up a body of support and love. Paul believed that the very future of the church depended on whether or not it would assume a corporate public life. His whole desire—both in his teaching of the church through his book of Ephesians and in his own personal engagement in public life as recorded in Acts and his letters to the Corinthians—was that the church would embrace public life and become assertively proactive in seeking to turn the Roman Empire upside down.

CONCLUSION

In one of his letters to the Corinthian church, Paul wrote, "For the kingdom of God depends not on talk but on power" (1 Cor 4:20). In Ephesians we see Paul systematically presenting what that single sentence alludes to in 1 Corinthians. The church is not to be about "talk," he argued. It is not about the task of maintaining a privatized faith, simply building up interiorized congregations and only sallying forth into the world to win converts to Christ. Paul knew that such insulation would lead to the marginalization, and eventually the disintegration, of the church.

Instead, what Paul did in his own ministry and what he urged on his congregations to do was to build the kingdom of God on *power*. He called them to move out into public life, living a compassionate and caring lifestyle different from the rest of society and working for the transformation of that society's systems into at least an approximation of the kingdom of God. In obedience to the vision Paul cast, that is in fact what the church did. And the result was the transformation of the Roman Empire into an increasingly Christianized society. It took the church nearly three hundred years to bring about that transformation. But that is exactly what they did. And it was all because Paul had given the church both a theology of public life and the courage to live out that public life in the Roman world.

Part Two

THE PRACTICE
OF POWER

7

BUILDING POWER
AROUND RELATIONSHIPS

IF YOU WANT TO BUILD RELATIONAL POWER in your church, mission organization or community, where do you begin? You begin with just one person. You begin by meeting with that person, sharing about the things that matter most to you and encouraging that person to share with you what matters are of greatest concern to him or her. You begin with individual meetings.

In my opinion the greatest leader of Judaism was Nehemiah. Just as Moses founded Israel and Jesus gave birth to the church and Paul led the church into its Gentile expansion, so Nehemiah was instrumental in the development of second-temple Judaism. Nehemiah's leadership after Jerusalem's walls were rebuilt led the Hebrew people to embrace the Deuteronomic reforms that eventually led to the rise of Judaism.[1] And it was the movement of Judaism that preserved Israel during the intertestamental period, gave rise to the Pharisee movement, became the foil for Jesus' ministry and maintained Judaism during the dispersion after the Roman destruction of Jerusalem. There would be no Judaism today if it had not been for Nehemiah.

All this began with Nehemiah's conversation with one man—his brother Hanani—in the Persian capital of Susa in April of 444 B.C. This was not a chitchat conversation; it was a *meeting*—one intentional meeting in which Nehemiah sought to discover the deepest passions and pain of his brother.

As a result of Nehemiah's drive to make that discovery, both Hanani's and Nehemiah's lives—and their nation—were permanently changed.

BUILDING RELATIONAL POWER FOR THE KINGDOM— JESUS AND PETER

Perhaps the biblical person most skilled in building relationships was Jesus. He built relationships intentionally and firmly. In fact one can argue that this was an essential and unique work of Jesus (along with his atoning death). In order to work toward the realization of the kingdom of God, Jesus needed to build a permanent organization. It would be the strength and integrity of that organization (first, a disciple band, then a church) that would perpetuate the effort to realize God's kingdom after Jesus had returned to the Father. And no such permanent organization could be built and sustained unless it was built on firm relationships.

Note how Jesus built those relationships. Each relationship between Jesus and another follows a similar pattern: Jesus would *commit* undivided, undistracted time to another person (whether it be a disciple, Zacchaeus or a leper), even when he would be in the midst of a crowd. He would *listen* to that person—not only to his words but also to the passion or pain that lay behind those words. Jesus would *affirm* that person so that she would feel loved and appreciated by him. Jesus would *challenge* that person to an action or decision, whether it was to take the next risky step of faith or to act on something he needed to do. A part of challenging that person would be to get her to *think through* her situation, often in the light of her relationship with Jesus or the call to jubilee. Finally, Jesus would often use the situation of an intense individual meeting with a person as an opportunity to *teach* that person. Nowhere does Jesus play these roles more evidently than in his relationship with Peter.

Matthew 14:22-33 describes the remarkable event of Jesus walking on the Sea of Galilee. While making a trip across the lake without Jesus, his disciples were caught in a storm. "And early in the morning [Jesus] came walking toward them on the sea. But when the disciples saw him walking on the sea, they were terrified" (Mt 14:25-26). As if this were not amazing enough,

Peter answered [Jesus], "Lord, if it is you, command me to come to you on the water." He said, "Come." So Peter got out of the boat, started walking on the water, and came toward Jesus. But when he noticed the strong wind, he became frightened, and beginning to sink, he cried out, "Lord, save me!" Jesus immediately reached out his hand and caught him, saying to him, "You of little faith, why did you doubt?" When they got into the boat, the wind ceased. (Mt 14:28-32)

Think of this incident as an individual meeting between Jesus and Peter held on a storm-tossed sea. Jesus is deeply listening to Peter. He is not simply listening to his request, "Command me to come to you on the water." He is listening to the heart's desire of a man who loves Jesus so much he wants to literally step out on faith into an impossible situation. By giving Peter permission to step onto the water, Jesus is encouraging him in this act of faith. When Peter doubts and begins to sink, Jesus challenges him by his tender response, "You of little faith, why did you doubt?" And once they both get into the safety of the boat, Peter's response, "Truly you are the Son of God," shows how much he is thinking through and learning from this "gentle stroll" with Jesus.

Matthew seems to pay particular attention to the nuances of the relationship between Jesus and Peter. In Matthew 16:13-28 Jesus asks the disciples who they believe he is. Peter answers, "You are the Messiah, the Son of the living God." Jesus' reaction to this openhearted response by Peter is profound.

> Blessed are you, Simon son of Jonah! For flesh and blood has not revealed this to you, but my Father in heaven. And I tell you, you are Peter, and on this rock I will build my church, and the gates of Hades will not prevail against it. I will give you the keys of the kingdom of heaven, and whatever you bind on earth will be bound in heaven, and whatever you loose on earth will be loosed in heaven. (Mt 16:17-19)

Can you imagine how Peter must have felt on hearing these words spoken by Jesus? *Affirmed* is too weak a word for the emotions that must have burst to life within Peter. But that emotion was soon followed by a significant challenge by Jesus when Peter sought to protect his Lord. Jesus had just shared with the disciples that naming him as Messiah didn't mean that he would be a conquering hero. The result of his being seen as Messiah was that he would undergo great persecution, suffering and even death in Jerusalem. Stunned by these words, Peter rebuked Jesus, "God forbid it, Lord! This must never happen to you" (Mt 16:22). It was those words that gained for Peter this stinging retort: "Get behind me, Satan! You are a stumbling block to me; for you are setting your mind not on divine things but on human things" (Mt 16:23).

From being proclaimed the rock upon which the church will be built to being called Satan—what a fall for Peter! But in that fall lies the challenge to Peter to think through his understanding of what it means to be a follower of a Messiah who would come to "give his life a ransom for many" (Mt 20:28).

These are just two of the many stories about Jesus intentionally investing quality time with Peter. Why did Jesus invest this kind of time in Peter? It was because he knew the kind of man Peter could become—the leader of the emerging Christian church. And Jesus' desire was to shape Peter into that kind of leader.

BUILDING RELATIONSHIPS THAT CHANGE THE WORLD
You can't hope to bring about significant change in a church, community, city or nation without building relationships. All truly transforming change must be built upon the creation and maintenance of strong relationships. But relationships that change people and systems are not warm, fuzzy, gentle, undemanding relationships. Jesus' relationships with his disciples and friends were intentional, demanding and called for commitment.

Relationships that will build power can't be created and maintained without a significant investment of time and energy. These relationships are built through intentionally selecting the people with whom you wish to build these relationships and then investing time in those people. That time investment is for determining whether a person has leadership potential that can be called forth—and then calling it forth! To accomplish that, your visiting must be intentional, selective and specific. This is done by what community organizers call "one-on-ones," or individual or relational meetings.

THE OBJECTIVE OF BUILDING RELATIONSHIPS
Your purpose in conducting individual meetings is to discover those who exhibit the potential or leadership capacity that encourages you to build a relationship with them. Your task is not to set your agenda down on them.

134

It is to learn from them *their* agenda—their pain, issues, problems, needs, joys, hopes and aspirations. You will not be able to organize a community toward change unless you take seriously the people's concerns.

In these face-to-face calls, you are seeking to build a possible working relationship with the people you're visiting. But you are also hoping to learn from them strategic information and insights about themselves and their community or church. These would include,

- What are their real concerns? What are their joys? Where do their pains lie, in regard to this city, community or church?

- Who do they perceive are significant actual leaders (as opposed to those who are simply titular leaders)?

- Who are those in their church or community who have a significant burden for that church or community, and what are their primary concerns?

To be effective, such calling must be done *in an organized manner.* As you call on a growing number of people, you will realize that you are hearing some common themes being named by a number of people, and you will find many people with a "fire in their belly." If you do not keep accurate records of each of your visits and have some means of collating the information you have so painstakingly gathered, the results of all that calling will be squandered.

Thus at regular points in your calling you need to be able to identify all the people on whom you have called who are particularly concerned with a given problem area (for example, their children's education). Based on that knowledge you have gathered, you will be able to call these people together to begin sharing their common concerns with each other. (We'll explore this further in the next chapter.)

Such calling must be done regularly. That means two things. *First, calling must be done often.* It is not an occasional task you need to perform; it must be done on a regular and predictable schedule. For example, I commit myself to making at least two calls each week (not including counseling or meeting appointments) on people I do not know well. That might include members of the congregation to which I belong, students I teach or people in the community in which I work. If you don't set a weekly schedule for yourself, you will never get around to doing these face-to-face visits, because the urgencies of a busy life will press in on you.

Second, calling must be repeated. Part of Jesus' success with Peter was that he didn't confine himself to just one call upon Peter. In the examples we studied earlier in this chapter, he encountered Peter twice. In reality, it was far, far more often than that. For your calls to be successful, they shouldn't be done only at the beginning of an organizing process. They should be done for the remainder of your life. And when you find a person who exhibits significant potential, you should call on her over and over again. If you are going to truly listen to this person, affirm her, challenge her and help her to think through her actions in light of the issues about which she is deeply concerned, that will mean repeated visits. You can't accomplish in a single call all you will want to do in building a relationship with this person.

There are different types of individual meetings—that is, meetings have differing objectives. There is the initial meeting in which you make the first acquaintance of the person and seek to ascertain if this person has leadership qualifications or other potential for this organizing effort. There are subsequent meetings when you seek to deepen the relationship with that person; you do this by getting to know him better and hearing more of his story. There may be meetings in which you are working with the person on a clearer articulation of her issues and sharing with her the reality that there are others in the organizing effort with the same issues. You might hold a meeting to learn whom he perceives as significant leaders in the community—particularly leaders not yet identified by the organizing effort. If the person is a pastor or a leader in her congregation, you might meet with her to more deeply involve that church in the organizing effort. There are many kinds of individual meetings, each appropriate to its own context.

WHOM TO CALL ON—AND HOW TO MEET THEM

If you are working in or deeply involved in a church, it is crucial to call on the *church people.* Doing individual meetings in your congregation is the surest way to get to know your church members, build firm and intentional relationships with them, discover their life concerns, and eventually equip them to organize themselves to address the deepest concerns, both in their church and in their daily lives. And frankly, the members of the congregation will love you for visiting them. People love to talk about themselves, want to have truly meaningful conversations with people regarding their concerns and want to be heard. If your church is made up of residents of its neighborhood, it is crucial that you meet individually with them, because they will become the leaders of outreach into that community. But even if your congregation is a commuter church, you need to visit with them, learning their joys, convictions and pains and why it is they choose to commute miles to your church.

Key people in your community are also crucial for you to build relationships with. Those key people include

- pastors and leaders of religious institutions
- political leaders (both elected and appointed) and those in the public sector
- business leaders (both of large corporations and of locally owned businesses)
- educators (both faculty and administration, from elementary to graduate schools)
- health care and service providers
- but most of all, *ordinary folks*

How do you make contact with people living or working in your church's neighborhood? The first and most important rule is that you need to follow whatever is appropriate to the culture in which you are working. For example, in Hispanic communities it would be acceptable to drop in for a visit. In Africa you would need the permission of the village or community "chief." In India, if you were a man you would never hold a personal visit with a woman. In the primarily Irish American community in which I once worked, the appropriate process was to conduct your visits at the local pub and build the acceptance that would allow you to visit elsewhere. In the typical American community, however, the most effective process is to make appointments.

It's an easy matter to make appointments with members of your church, because you already have credibility. And normally you can get appointments with those in the public sector—pastors, political leaders, business leaders, educators, health care and service providers—because they feel they need to be responsive to the public. But the case can be different with "ordinary folks." With such people, you may have insufficient credibility to get an appointment. One of the best ways to build that credibility is through referrals and credentialing.

Building such credibility is begun by visiting people with whom you already have credibility, such as members of your church living in the neighborhood, pastors who know you, or teachers and administrators in the schools where your children are enrolled. During your visit, ask them for names of people they would recommend you contact. Usually they are more than glad to supply names. Better yet, have them credential you—that is, have them telephone those people to alert them that they will be hearing from you and urging them to agree to visit with you.

There is one strategy I would strongly urge you *not* to use—door-to-door contacts. Going door to door is extremely unproductive because you are basically invading people's privacy. Even worse, it reduces you in their eyes to little more than a salesperson, and they will treat you as such. Even if you get into the home, you will run into a wall of sales resistance.

When you visit, should you go alone or visit in pairs or teams? Well, you are trying to build a relationship with the person you are visiting. If a team or pair of you calls on that person, it turns the call into a formal interview, not a shared visit. Likewise, taking notes converts the call into an interview—and honest sharing will plummet. Also, the visit should be face to face, because phone calls or e-mails radically reduce the personal nature of the call. Remember, you are seeking to build a relationship with that person, not to gather data, so you need to do all those things that best build relationships.

But what about calling on someone of the opposite sex? The call still should be face to face, but it would be best to conduct it in a public setting rather than in the privacy of that person's home. I call the Starbucks coffee shop near my church my "second office" because I conduct so many individual meetings there. It is the perfect place to meet with someone of the opposite sex—a public setting that allows a private conversation at a table over two cups of coffee.

How to Conduct an Individual Meeting

Preparation. Before you visit the person you have selected, there are some preparatory tasks you need to do. Obviously you ought to have contacted him or her and made an appointment to meet. When you make that appointment, request the length of time you would like the meeting to be (normally between a half-hour and an hour). *Never* exceed that time limit, unless you have asked for and received permission to extend the time.

You would bring with you the form on which you plan to report on that meeting. However, it is important that you leave the form out in your automobile and not bring it in with you. You do not want to take any notes at the meeting (except as noted below), because taking notes will turn the meeting into a survey and make it harder to build the relationship. It is acceptable to write down a date—an appointment on your calendar that the two of you agree on, or a name or address.

Introduction. If you greet the person at his door, tell him who you are and the name of your organization (not the community organization but the organization you represent, such as a church). Remind him of the appointment you have made with him, and ask if you can come in. If you have been referred to him or have been credentialed by someone, be sure to mention that fact. Perhaps this introduction could be something like this: "Hi. I'm Bob Linthicum, and I'm one of the pastors at First Presbyterian Church. I called you a few days ago for an appointment, and you said this would be a good time for us to visit. Jane Fitzsimmons suggested that I visit with you, and I think she contacted you about me." (The person being visited here acknowledges your and Jane's contact and invites you in. Both of you take your seats and the conversation continues.)

After you have been seated, explain the purpose of your visit. This is best done by sharing how you became involved in making visits like this one and why building relationships through visiting is important to you. If you can do this by telling a story, so much the better. It may go something like this: "As I mentioned, I'm from First Presbyterian Church, and we have been in this neighborhood for seventy-five years now. But we've come to realize that we haven't been very good neighbors. We have kept to ourselves and nurtured our own members, but we haven't gotten involved in the neighborhood problems that seem to be getting worse here. A month ago one of our church leaders got accosted in the parking lot and robbed, and we decided something had to be done about the growing problems of our neighborhood—including crime. So we decided that the first thing we needed to do was to start talking to our neighbors. And Jane Fitzsimmons, who's a member of First Church, said she thought you were a really key person for us to visit. So that's why I'm here—to get to know you better and to see whether we have some common concerns."

Obviously almost all of the above only has to be presented on the first visit. After that, the person will know you, and when you visit again, you can simply get down to business.

The body of the visit. The body of the visit is, of course, different for each call. What is contained below is important material to cover in an early call. You'll most likely not deal with all of the following in a first call—nor should you attempt to do so.

The first portion of the body of the visit (and this may be all you do in the first visit) is to simply get to know people and to discover what they really care about.[2] The way you do this is to ask open-ended questions, to listen and to probe gently. You should ask questions around people's concerns, issues and worries and around their interests, joys and passions. You can ask questions to help them share their vision for the community or city, to articulate their primary values or to share gifts. The best way for them to do this is by telling a story (that is, they will have the easiest time articulating concerns, passions or convictions by telling a story rather than abstractly articulating it).

On an initial visit, I have found that one of the easiest ways to get people to share is to ask them the question, "How long have you lived in this community?" (or, if it is a church visit, "How long have you been a member of our church?"). There are really only two ways they can answer that question: "a long time" or "a short time."

If they answer the question with "a long time," I then ask them, "How have you seen this community (or church) change over those years?" With a question like that, the likelihood is that they will be off and running as they talk about the community's or church's changes. The very concerns they choose to mention will tell you a great deal about their priorities, values and desires.

If, on the other hand, they answer the question with "a short time," I then ask, "What caused you to select this neighborhood (church) to move into? There are 138 neighborhoods (churches) in our city. Why did you choose this one?" When they give their answer (for example, "I moved here because

I heard the schools were far better than they are in other parts of our city, and I wanted the best education for my children"), then ask them, "Have you found that to be true? Are you pleased with the quality of education your children are receiving?" Again they likely will be off and running as they talk about the community. And from what they say, you will have a good idea what their priorities, values and desires are.

The best way to get people sharing their joys and concerns is through stories. The way you ask questions will either point people toward the telling of stories or away from that. In the illustration given in the previous paragraph regarding the parent moving to a neighborhood because of the high reputation of the schools, you could get the person to share some stories by asking questions like, "Can you give me an example of how your children have responded to the education provided here?" or "Would you share an incident when you felt your children were treated unfairly in school?"

The person's responses to these initial questions could lead to further questions. For example, you can ask them directly what they like or dislike about living in this community, what brings them joy or what causes them anger, what most bothers them about living in this neighborhood or what most bothers them about raising their children here. As you ask these questions, you seek to identify the issues they feel most strongly about, and you look for clues as to how passionately the person feels about those concerns. Seek to find out where people's passions lie and how deeply they feel about them.

IDENTIFYING COMMUNITY LEADERS

It is a community's informal leadership that gives shape, direction and focus to a neighborhood. That informal leadership is rarely elected or appointed; it simply evolves as community members acknowledge and affirm that leadership.

There are certain distinct roles informal leadership takes. Some are *gatekeepers.* They provide primary leadership to the community and are the "elders" whose wisdom others respect. Others are that neighborhood's *caretakers,* who provide care and support to the people of the neighborhood, especially the children. Some are *flak-catchers.* They run the informal communication network of the community through which everyone keeps informed. And others are the *brokers* of the community, who have active working connections to the political, economic and values-articulating and sustaining systems of the city, and who can therefore get things done in the neighborhood because of who they know rather than what they know.[3]

Discovering these leaders is crucial to the success of community organizing. If they are actively involved in and cooperating with the organizing effort, they can greatly enhance the acting out of relational power in that community or city. If they are opposed to the organizing effort, they will act as a significant brake on it.

Identifying these people and then calling on them and building relationships with them is strategic. Questions that can help identify them are as follows.

To identify the gatekeeper, you might ask a question like, "If you wanted a decision made by this neighborhood on what to do with an empty lot, who could bring the neighbors to a decision?"

To find the caretaker, ask, "If you had a terrible crisis at 2:00 a.m. and no one from your family was available, who would you contact in this neighborhood that you know would come to your aid?" (Incidentally, if the answer is "911," that tells you a great deal about the lack of community in your area.)

A question to help identify the flak-catcher might be, "If you wanted to communicate to one of your neighbors that he needs to take better care of his lawn, whom would you contact who could build community pressure to get that neighbor to conform?"

To identify the broker, ask, "If you had a bad pothole in the street and the city wasn't getting around to fix it, who could get the city out here quickly to fix it?"

Identifying those who care. Is the person upon whom you're calling a person who deeply cares about the future of this community? A way to determine that is to ask a question like this: "When you think about living in this neighborhood, what breaks your heart?" *How* the person answers that question is as important as *what* she says. If she displays a great deal of surprise at being asked that question, has trouble articulating an answer or answers in a hesitant manner, that likely means that nothing breaks her heart. If, on the other hand, she has no trouble answering the question (probably because she has thought about it before) and answers with conviction and engagement, this is likely a person with "a fire in her belly." This is a person you want in the organizing effort.

Motivating involvement in the organizing effort. As soon as you feel some receptivity on the part of the one on whom you're calling, you should share ways that person's values, vision and concerns could be powerfully addressed by participating in the community's organization. You can do that by highlighting those elements of the organizing process that relate to his or her story and concerns. You might share your story of how involvement in organizing personally, or on the part of your church or group, empowered you or others to make a difference in the community. Be sure to speak from your own experience, not as an expert.

In this portion of the body of your visit it is important that you share the great potential of relational power. Do so, not by speaking philosophically or even biblically about it, but by simply sharing your story. There is nothing to compare with a person saying, "Once I was blind, but now I see!" It is important to share relevant portions of your own story with the person. There may be events that happened in your life that are similar to or connect with or relate to the life experiences he or she has shared with you. And your disclosure of information about your own life may encourage him or her to share even more deeply. Such sharing is particularly strategic if you are able to demonstrate how your participation in the use of relational power or involvement in community organizing resolved the difficulty you shared. This will show organizing at work to the person whom you're visiting.

CLOSING THE VISIT

How you end a meeting is important. You need to do several things to guarantee that the meeting results in more than simply an enjoyable visit.

Get a commitment. Ask the person to make some sort of commitment. That might be asking, "If I find other people in the community (or congregation) who share concerns or interests similar to yours, would you be willing to get together with them so we can discuss what we might do about these shared concerns?" This might mean asking the person to come to a gathering that has already been organized. It might mean asking her to attend a planning meeting. Whatever it is, ask the one you're visiting to take a next step. And if his answer is yes, tell him you will get back to him regarding such a meeting, and ask him how he would prefer to be contacted (home phone, business phone, e-mail) and the best times to contact him.

Get a referral. Ask her if there is anyone she would recommend you visit. This should be a person like herself whom she knows is actively engaged in the community or has a concern about involvement in public life or is highly knowledgeable about the community or church. Incidentally this is the one time in the visit when it is acceptable for you to write. Ask her for that person's address and phone number, and write it down.

Ask for credentialing. This is as important as a referral. Even if you casually know the person he refers you to, ask him if he would contact that person (preferably face to face, but if that is impossible, even by phone or e-mail) to alert that person that you will be contacting him or her for an appointment and to assure that person that this will be a pleasant and profitable visit. Ask the one who will be credentialing you when that contact will be made. Ostensibly you ask this because you don't want to contact the referral before the credentialing occurs. But the primary reason for asking for the date of contact is to reinforce the commitment you are requesting from the one you are contacting.

Take your leave. You have now come to the end of your call. Thank the person for her time, remind her you'll be getting back to her, and take your leave.

All of the material listed above in the body and close of an individual meeting would not be done in *every* individual meeting. Each meeting is shaped by its purpose and primary emphasis. But these are some of the important elements of early calls on a person with whom you are seeking to build a power relationship.

COMPLETING THE INDIVIDUAL MEETING

Even though you have now left the person with whom you have just visited, you haven't yet completed your individual meeting. Get into your car and drive around the corner. Park the car and fill out the information form you brought with you. The form need not be complex; I use a single sheet of paper and list at the top the date and the name, address, phone number, e-mail address and occupation or profession of the person I've visited (most of that can be filled out ahead of time). The body of the form simply consists of three divisions of the paper with plenty of white space. The first division is "joys, values, vision." The second division is "concerns, issues." The third is "other comments." Usually in "other comments" I place the commitments the person made to me. The bottom of the paper has a place for the name, address and phone number of those I have been referred to, and whether the person upon whom I had just called will credential me.

I urge you to fill out that form as soon after the meeting as possible. You will be amazed by how quickly you will forget details if you don't write them down. If you have several calls in a row, allot the time *between* the calls to fill out the form on the completed call; otherwise the chance of confusing elements of the two calls is extremely high. Believe me; I'm speaking from experience!

Once you get home, program the information on the form into the data bank you have set up on your computer so you can easily cross-reference people regarding their concerns, issues, convictions, visions, geographical communities, vocations and group connections (like their church or their membership with the local rose growers society).[4]

WHAT NOT TO DO

What you don't do in a call is as important as what you do. Don't use that call to share your faith or to evangelize. The reason you don't want to share your faith at such a meeting is because it compromises the meeting and creates distrust—and the entire process of creating relational power is built on trust.

If the opportunity arises in an individual meeting to share your faith and you do so, the person you are visiting may interpret your sharing as a betrayal of the commitments you made in securing the meeting with him. That is, he may think, "Oh, now I get it. All this talk about being interested in hearing my concerns and learning from me was a way of setting me up to try to get me to become a Christian."

But what if a person directly asks you about your faith? Even in such an instance (and it has happened to me numerous times), I say, "I would very much like to share with you my faith because it is the most important thing in my life. But that is not what I told you this meeting was about when I asked to visit with you, and I don't want to break my promise to you. So if you would like to set up a meeting when you and I can talk about our respective faiths, I would be eager to do that. But I don't want to talk about that in this meeting."

By answering this way, you have preserved both your integrity and the integrity of the meeting, and you have now placed the decision with the individual you are visiting. At this point, he can do one of several things. He can say, "All right, let's talk about it at another meeting," and you can make a date with him right then. Or he can answer, "No, I don't care to go further with this." Again, that lets him be in charge. Or he can respond, "I really want to talk about it now." If that's his response, you can ask, "Is it all right with you if we change the focus of this visit from what I originally contracted with you and take more time than what we originally agreed to?" If he says, "Yes," (which he likely would, given his request), then *he* has made the choice, and he likely will not feel manipulated. You will have protected both your integrity and that of the organizing effort of which you are a part.

Of course, the work of building relationships of power is not completed with a single visit. It has just begun! It is unlikely that you'll get through the entire calling format on one visit (and you should probably not try to do so). If there seems to be interest and potential there, you will want to go back for further visits and the nurturing of the relationship with that person. More importantly, you will want to move that person beyond individual meetings with you to being involved in house meetings, participating in an action team, conducting action research and working with others to bring about substantive change in her church, community or city. In due time you will be training this person to do individual meetings with her friends and associates as well. And you will go on to do many more meetings with many more people. In fact, if you are successful in building relational power, you will discover that about half of the time you spend working on building such power will be spent in nurturing people. And this you will primarily do through the vehicle of individual meetings.

TRANSFORMING YOUR MINISTRY THROUGH RELATIONAL MEETINGS

In the first three months that I was pastor at Edgewater Presbyterian Church in Chicago in 1969, I committed one day a week to conducting individual meetings among both church members and community leaders. As I met with people and heard their hopes and concerns, I began to realize how out of touch the elected leadership of my church had become—even with their own church members. So I challenged them to join me in calling. To my utter amazement and delight, they agreed.

As I began my fourth month at that church, I trained fifty-two of its leaders to do individual meetings. About a quarter of them called on our 550 members. And all the others called on community leaders and residents, with about half of those people calling on ordinary people and the other half targeting pastors, political leaders, business owners and managers, educators, and health care and service providers.

Over the next six months these leaders conducted relational meetings with more than two thousand people in our inner-city community and our church. We gathered twice each month to have dinner together, to spend time in biblical reflection and to report what we were discovering from our visits. Gradually a profile of both our church and the Edgewater community began to form. And we were amazed at the similarities in the two profiles. We had always considered ourselves to be an upper-middle-class congregation, but we began to realize that the daily concerns of our members bore a striking resemblance to the everyday concerns of the poorer residents of Edgewater and its leaders. Out of that realization our leaders created a mission design for our church that set the future for our ministry both for my tenure there and for many years after. And it moved my church out into that community in powerful ways that have brought about a people's organization that continues today, has reshaped the economic and cultural life of that community, has built considerable political power vested in the people and has built significant strength in that church.

All these changes happened to a church and its community because our leaders were willing to commit one day each week to sitting down with people to listen and to learn from them. This is relational power tapped through individual meetings!

8

ORGANIZING FOR COMMUNITY ACTION

AS I REACHED THE BROW OF THE HILL one rainy day in November 1990, I could see the slum of Carton City lying below in the lush river valley of Nairobi, Kenya. Although my eyes could not yet tell the condition of the slum, my nostrils could. I could clearly smell the stench of burned and charred buildings. A great fire had most certainly occurred recently in Carton City.

The Reverend David Ashiko and I began down the winding path, and as we approached Carton City, I could begin to see the extent of the damage. Scores of homes lay before us roofless and with scorched walls, many burnt to the ground. When we arrived in the slum, the people gathered around us, eager to tell their story to anyone who would listen.

Carton City, they told us, was an old slum—one of the first in the city of Nairobi—created soon after Kenya won freedom from the British. Dating back generations, it was constructed on government land in the floodplain of the Nairobi River, close to the military airport. Its inhabitants, primarily poor and uneducated freedom fighters in Kenya's struggle for independence, had simply squatted on that government land, seeking to scratch a living from its rich alluvial soil. It was named Carton City because so many of its people lived in cardboard cartons with sheet-metal roofs.

The government had tolerated the existence of Carton City for decades. But recently it had decided the slum had to go. Only the night before, the police had entered Carton City during an intense tropical storm. They roused all the people from their beds and made the families gather their belongings and stand in the pouring rain. Then, waving batons and firing pistols in the air, the police forced the father of each family to set fire to his own house. The people stood there helplessly in the pouring rain, watching their simple homes burn to the ground. For many it was the bitter end. They were defeated, broken, homeless, the men exposed before their families for the helpless victims they were. The people of Carton City had no place to go and were unwanted where they were.

I returned to Carton City sixteen months later. What now greeted my eyes was a significantly transformed community. Solid two- and three-room mud-brick houses filled the slum. The dirt streets were swept clean, with no litter anywhere except in designated pits some distance from the homes. Behind each home was a pit latrine so that each family had its own toilet, and community showers had been installed throughout the complex. There was both a piggery and a fowl farm in operation, and a large vegetable garden provided food for all in the slum and for sale. Carton City had radically changed. What had happened?

When I asked, I received a very simple answer: "Clement Adongo came to be with us!" Adongo was one of a team of four organizers led by the person who had originally accompanied me into Carton City, David Ashiko. Ashiko led World Vision Kenya's community organizing effort, Urban Advance, which was developing throughout Nairobi. When Ashiko accompanied me into Carton City in November 1990, we both agreed that this was a slum in which we should begin the Urban Advance organizing effort. Ashiko, an accomplished organizer, worked there part time until he employed and trained Adongo. And then Adongo began working in Carton City full time.

Adongo started by entering into the lives of the people of Carton City. He spent innumerable hours conducting individual meetings with them—asking questions, listening to their stories and learning about their lives. He heard that many of the men had fought for freedom from Britain, that there were no jobs after independence and that the people had come to squat in Carton City, hoping for day labor at the nearby military base. He learned that many of the women had resorted to begging, stealing or prostitution to support their families. He listened to their pain and frustration and their sense of abandonment and even betrayal by the government they had helped bring to power. And Adongo allowed his heart to be broken by the things that were breaking the hearts of "his" people.

Once he had built trusting relationships with a majority of the residents of Carton City, Adongo began gathering them together into house meetings. In those small groups, they told their stories, shared each other's pain and then began to talk about how they could make Carton City a better place to live.

Almost immediately the people began to identify what they had to do. Before they could act powerfully in the Kenyan political context, they had to begin building economic power. They started small. They created three income-generating projects, and with the production and selling of clothes, baskets, charcoal and furniture, a stream of income began flowing into the community. The only member of the community who could read and write besides Adongo went into a bank for the first time in her life; there she opened an interest-bearing account for the monies the community was generating. The people decided to build the latrines and community showers and then created the two farms and vegetable garden.

Then a new deputy chief was appointed for the district of Nairobi in which Carton City lay. And he visited Carton City. Taking note of the people's improved standard of living, he decided he wanted some of it. Soon he informed the residents of Carton City that they had to pay a new tax. But the people discovered that there was no new tax. This was simply a way for the deputy chief to steal from the people. So the citizens of Carton City refused to pay.

One night the police entered the slum again. Under the orders of the deputy chief, they set fire to selected houses. But this time the people didn't meekly stand by and watch their homes burn. Instead of cowering in fear, the residents of Carton City rose up in anger. The community descended *en masse* upon the government, and there demanded and got an audience with the chief, the immediate superior of the deputy chief. They issued a complaint against the man and demanded retribution. But the chief refused to cooperate. So the community leaders went to the district commissioner, threatening to reveal the whole scandal to the newspapers. Immediately the district commissioner removed the deputy chief from his post and paid for the destroyed homes. And the people tasted significant victory for the first time against Nairobi's "principalities and powers."

But the people didn't leave it there. Adongo got the people to reflect on what they had learned from this incident and on what their next steps in dealing with the government should be. They decided to take two crucial steps. First, they would build permanent homes for each other. By Kenyan law, the building of a permanent home on unclaimed land "stakes a claim" to that land for its owner. Second, they notified the government that the slum would monitor every meeting of the District Development Committee (the local legislative body) to hold the government accountable. A Carton City representative has attended every meeting since. And the people have taken a number of actions to be sure their voice is heard.

The community then created its own construction firm and began building permanent homes for each other. These homes are substantial by Kenyan standards—two and three rooms, constructed of permanent brick and appointed with glass windows and wooden doors. One by one the people replaced their cardboard huts with these new homes.

The story of Carton City is a clear example of what community organizing is meant to do as it teaches people how to use power. The success of the people of Carton City is a clear manifestation of the Iron Rule of organizing: "Never do for others what they can do for themselves." But God's people can most effectively practice this Iron Rule when we follow the strategy "power precedes program."

POWER PRECEDES PROGRAM

Our tendency as Christians is to program absolutely everything. Think how programmed the church is. Committees, boards, task forces—we build our life and ministry on programs.

But organizing operates on an entirely different (and I think a far more biblical) rationale. It works on the premise that the way to bring about significant change is not to build a program but to build power. The way to enable people to "do for themselves" is by enabling them to work together to empower each other, not by developing a program that only strengthens their dependency.

Think of how Jesus built the church. He launched no programs; he created no committees; he developed no projects. Instead he invested himself in twelve men and seven women.[1] He spent time with them, listened to them, affirmed them, challenged them, made them think and taught them. He built relationships with them, both as individuals and as a group. And he motivated—in fact, pushed—them to "do for themselves." He had them preach, heal the sick, cast out demons, raise the dead, walk on water. "You . . . will do greater works than [mine]," he told them (Jn 14:12). And he did this, not just for individuals, but also as a community together. In other words what Jesus was doing was building a community of power. His essential task was to build his disciples into people of power so that once he had ascended to the Father they could build a community of faith throughout the world. What Jesus was about was the building of a permanent organization, and he did that through the building of relationships.

Power is rarely built through a program. It is built through intentional relationships that knit together the fabric of a community—an organization. And once that organization is sufficiently built, *then* that organization can address the issues and concerns of the people in significant ways, because it has built the power base to do so.

How is power built? All we need do is refer back to the way Nehemiah built the power of a particularly powerless Jewish people. Think of all the steps Nehemiah took to build a powerful Jewish community, as we examined them in chapter five. He *built relationships* with key people necessary for rebuilding both the walls and the corporate life of the Jewish people. From his individual meetings with the people, he *identified leaders* with strong leadership capabilities. He *identified the problems and opportunities* the people were facing. He *"rubbed raw" the problem*, getting the community to talk about the problem. He also *conducted a power analysis*, researching which system leaders would be cooperative and which would oppose the rebuilding.

Nehemiah also publicly *turned the problem into the issue*, so the people could act on it. Then the people *developed the implementing strategy* and determined a *clear objective*, identifying specific *targets*[2] for the work, a *desired response* for each target, followed up with particular *actions*[3] needed to achieve *the win*—the rebuilding of the walls.

So the people *organized and implemented the strategy*. As the work continued, they *reflected often* to adapt to changing situations. They *successfully completed each action* and *evaluated* every action and the lessons learned. They *celebrated* their victories and *set the next objectives and actions.* Ultimately, Nehemiah *built a strong organization,* a relational community of people that could act powerfully by acting collectively. In other words, Nehemiah was building a power organization.

FOUR PIVOTAL STRATEGIES

The book of Nehemiah magnificently demonstrates how to build a power organization upon intentional relationships. By studying it, we can discern the steps that a pastor, church, lay leader or community worker must take to build a people of power (rather than a programmed people). But our discussion is not complete without reflecting on the four pivotal strategies by which we can organize for community action: individual meetings, house meetings, research actions and actions.

Individual meetings. I have dedicated an entire chapter to individual meetings (chapter seven) to give you a sense of how important these are. To build relational power, one must build it person by person by person. Individual meetings are the foundation upon which organizing a people of power is built. It is the first thing you do. And it is the continuing thing you do. Every pastor's ministry, every teacher's profession, every worker's job, every student's day would be transformed if we only spent time intentionally visiting, listening to, affirming, challenging and getting people to think through the causes of the pain and the joy in their lives. Biblical relational power cannot be built except upon the foundation of people sharing their deepest concerns.

House meetings. The second major strategy is that of house meetings. By *house meetings,* we mean meetings of a small enough group of people that they can meet comfortably in someone's parlor or family room. A house meeting is seven to fifteen people gathering in a church basement, at a restaurant, in a school classroom or in a house to share their deepest concerns and hopes and to reflect together about what those gathered at that meeting can do about it. A house meeting can be made up of people gathered *geographically* (that is, the people with whom you have held individual meetings in a given neighborhood), *institutionally* (people from the same church), or *by issue* (people who have identified a specific problem as their highest concern).

153

In essence a house meeting is an expanded individual meeting; it can accomplish in a group setting what is accomplished in a one-on-one meeting. However, the house meeting should not be seen as a substitute for individual meetings. Both types of meetings are necessary for building relational power.

Like an individual meeting, a house meeting provides the opportunity for people to share their pain and their hopes, to tell their stories, to express their convictions and to make commitments. But unlike an individual meeting, a house meeting allows people to share their pain and hopes with many people. This type of meeting moves beyond the one-on-one of the interviewee and the interviewer. And that is the genius of house meetings: they result in people building solidarity and community together.

Conducting a house meeting provides the opportunity for people who might otherwise never talk to each other to share their concerns and hopes and to hear each other's stories. Even for people who meet each other socially every week, the house meeting provides an opportunity to share at a far deeper level about things that really matter (for example, our children's education, the increase in crime in our community, the problems of growing old in this society). Most meetings in church are social or are oriented around the conduct of the business of the church, but few are substantive and focus on issues that really matter to people. By its very nature, the house meeting is designed to move people beyond superficiality, individualism and piety to the intense sharing of issues that really matter—and to do that through the telling of stories.

However, that happens only if the one leading the house meeting asks agitational questions. The chief objective of the pastor, community organizer or community worker leading such a meeting is to agitate people. But agitation is not irritation. It is not seeking to annoy, to attack, to confront or to be sarcastic. Agitation is the effort to "rub raw" the concerns and particularly the *passions* of people by asking those hard questions that will make them think and express their feelings to each other. It is asking questions like, "How does that make you feel when you're treated that way?" "Why do we feel we can't fight City Hall?" "What keeps you awake at night, worrying?" "What makes you angry?" "When you look at the kids in our neighborhood, what breaks your heart?" or "Why are we reluctant to do something about it?" Only agitational questions will cause people to move beyond their comfort zones and begin both to share their anger and to build the resolve to act together regarding the problems articulated at that house meeting.

The genius of house meetings is built on the turning of "hot anger" into "cold anger." Christians have a real problem with accepting anger within themselves or others, feeling it isn't very Christlike. But, along with love and as a natural extension of love, it is the primary emotion attributed to God—and God's anger is almost always directed toward either injustice or spiritual unfaithfulness. Paul, who understood anger very well, commands us, "Be angry but do not sin; do not let the sun go down on your anger, and do not make room for the devil" (Eph 4:26-27).

Paul is telling us that anger is a part of life, and therefore it is important to be in touch with your anger. What angers you about injustice is triggered by similar injustice you experienced in your past. Sharing your stories with others both grounds your anger (so you understand it better) and connects you with others of similar experience or conviction. "Sinning" in your anger is holding onto your anger as hot anger, letting it seethe inside you but not doing anything about it. To fan the anger within you but to do nothing about it internalizes that anger, turning it inward on yourself, and thus does damage to you. Or the other alternative is to refuse to acknowledge the anger you feel and thus submerge it inside you. To do so allows that anger, particularly if it is recurring, to move into your subconscious and to thus become personally destructive. To handle anger in these ways is to "sin."

Paul continues, "Do not let the sun go down on your anger." By that he means the way to deal with your anger is to share it with others and to find allies who feel the same way. If you let the sun go down on your anger, it will become a festering wound within you and will harm you and those whom you love the most. But if you share that anger and the injustice that caused it, you will begin to move in healthy ways to deal with it by organizing with others to remove the injustice. In other words, Paul is saying that you must turn your hot anger into cold, deliberate anger that works toward a solution.

Finally Paul concludes, "And do not make room for the devil." You make room for the devil to control you when you internalize, deny or suppress your anger. God's way to deal with your anger is to join with others of common anger to work toward change in the situation or in the systems whose injustice caused the anger. The accomplishment of this task is the primary purpose of the house meeting.

Unlike individual meetings that never cease, house meetings are temporary. They are a transitional step between individual meetings and the involvement of people in ongoing issue-based groups within the larger organizing effort. But house meetings are a very necessary step; without them, people would rarely move from an individual complaint to joint action with others.

To build a strong organization of a community and its churches, the organizing effort needs to provide the means by which the people can be involved in hands-on action in the areas of their expressed concerns. The way most community and broad-based organizations do that is by the formation of "action teams," with each team dedicated to one specific area of concern. Thus you could have one action team dealing with crime and gangs, another with public education, another with housing and homelessness and another with jobs and unemployment. The understanding is that each action team does the research and groundwork necessary to prepare for action in that area of concern. But the entire organization and all its member churches and institutions have an obligation to support that action team in any action the organization approves.[4]

The house meeting is a vehicle by which people can move from an individual meeting to an action team by meeting together to share concerns, receive support, build relationships and decide to actually do something about the issue that matters most to them. This in turn leads to the third basic strategy of organizing—the strategy of research actions.

Research actions. Each action team in a community or broad-based organization exists to do the research and groundwork necessary to prepare for action in its area of concern and then to manage and coordinate the efforts of the organization to carry out actions.

A community organization's action team conducts a research action to gather information or to test the will or intention of a public or private official. *Action* is a technical term in the field of organizing that refers to an intentional and deliberate act on the part of the community organization to require a response of an official or leader on the issue the organization has determined needs to be acted upon. A *research action*, therefore, is an intentional and deliberate act that is done in order to provide information to that organization.

For example, the community organization might want to propose particular legislation to bring about a reform in public education. The action might be a public meeting at which those legislators present are asked to support the legislation. A research action, on the other hand, might be an intermediate step to find out if given legislators would attend that public meeting. If the research actions indicated that most legislators could not attend that meeting because of a scheduling conflict, the community organization might heed that research and decide to change the date of the meeting.

The purpose of a research action, therefore, is to gather information or to test the will of an official or leader. With the information gathered from that research, the community organization's action team can then sharpen the issue and make a more informed determination of who should be the "target" (the person targeted by the organization's action who has the authority to make the decision the organization is requesting be made), what the objective of the proposed action should be, what the action should be, what strategy would be most likely to succeed, who will support the proposed action and who will oppose it. In other words, the research action supplies information the organization needs to make the decisions that will most likely meet with success.

There are many kinds of research actions. The first kind is the gathering of statistical and technical data. Having sufficient and relevant data is essential. When the community organization's leaders meet with those who represent the political or economic powers, the community and church leaders must be able to demonstrate that they know as much about the subject matter as the target does. When the target realizes how well informed these leaders are, she will more likely enter into negotiation with them because other alternative responses won't work.

A second kind of research action is to meet with individual officials of unilateral institutions. This would include legislators, administrators of public institutions (for example, the superintendent of a school district) and corporate officials (the vice president of a corporation or the bishop of a diocese). Such meetings would be for the purpose of gaining support for the action, for soliciting information or for building a working relationship.

A third kind of research action is that of meeting with a delegation or an assembled body to seek support. That might include a legislative committee, a board of directors or an elected body. Unlike an action that would demand a particular kind of response, this would be an exploratory meeting to share the problem or issue, ask for support or advice, or request commitment. But the primary purpose of such a research action is to find out how this body would respond to this issue and to initiate a working relationship.

How should a research action be undertaken?

1. The action team needs to determine what the issue and their tentative action would be. The research action would test that tentative action or issue to see if it is indeed workable and winnable.

2. The action team should determine the research needed to test that tentative action. Is it data we need to gather? If so, what? Is it legislators we need to influence? Is it officials with whom we need to build working relationships? If so, who?

3. The research must be undertaken and the results gathered.

4. The gathered information and responses are examined, and from that examination, the actual action, objective, target and campaign is created.

The gathered information might lead to conducting a power analysis. A power analysis is an examination of how power *actually* flows in a given situation, as opposed to how it theoretically flows according to some organizational chart. In light of the information gathered, simply write on a whiteboard or flip chart the names of the people who your research indicates are the key decision makers. Then determine which of these people talk with whom to move toward a decision. Ask questions like, "Who goes to whom to deal with an issue? Who is most pivotal in the making of a strategic decision? Who would we need to get to support us? What would be the most likely strategy to get that person's support?" Draw lines from strategic decision makers to other strategic decision makers. He who gets the most lines wins—that's the key person you need to influence.

Actions. "The action is in the reaction." This statement captures the heart of a public action. An action is an intentional and deliberate act on the part of a community organization to require a response of a target on the issue the organization has determined needs to be acted on. An action is therefore the heart of organizing; it seeks to call a government or business official to accountability.

In essence the objective of an action is to get the target to react to the demand the community organization is making of him. He is being faced with a demand of the people that requires him to make a choice. How the target reacts to the community organization's action determines how the organization will react to the target and that target's institution.

The reaction of the target can take several forms. The first is to agree with the demand. That agreement can take three forms. The target may accept the specific demand placed before her. Or she may propose changes in the demand that are acceptable to the community organization. Or she may propose an alternative that accomplishes what the community organization wants accomplished but goes about it a different way. Of course simply getting agreement from the target doesn't mean the situation is resolved. One can say "yes" but never follow through. (One must be particularly culturally sensitive here because in some cultures it is considered rude to give a direct "no" but is considered appropriate to agree and then do nothing.) To make sure a "yes" is truly a yes, it is incumbent on the action team to set a date for the issue to be resolved, let the target know the people's organization will monitor the situation and then hold her accountable to fulfill her agreement.

The second reaction is to reject the demand. That too can take three forms. First, the target can simply say, "No, I won't do it," and take the consequences (loss of credibility with the electorate, loss of votes, loss of business). The second is to "blow smoke"—that is, to seek to obfuscate the response by saying, "I can't do it because . . ." If the community organization and its action team have done adequate research, they will be able to dismantle that excuse. The third is to say, "I need to study your proposal." That is the trickiest response of all. It can mean one of two things: that the person and his staff really do need to study the proposal to determine its feasibility, or that the target is politely saying "no" (that is, to apparently study it but never intend to make a decision on it). The community organization must immediately decide which study response the target is actually making by pushing for a date for a further meeting and a final answer. If the target genuinely needs to study it, he will gladly set a date. If this is a way to say "no" without saying "no," he will refuse to set a date. In such a case, the organization must proclaim to the gathered body and the media that the official's answer is, in reality, "no."

If the response of the target is no, it now becomes incumbent on the community organization to take the next step. How will the people respond to the reaction of the target? Of course, an effective organization will not quickly reveal its plans; rather it will keep the target on pins and needles by saying, "You will hear from us later." Then the organization and its action team will carefully plan their next move with the ultimate objective being to get the target or the target's superior to accept the demand of the people.

In reality, an action is an exercise of power. It is the ultimate act of power of a relational organization; it uses power in such a way that it declares to the target that relationship with that organization, its constituent institutions, its thousands or tens of thousands of people and all whom that organization influences will be denied the target if she ignores those matters most important to the people. It is calling that official to accountability before the people who elected him to office or who supply the tax dollars to pay his salary, or who purchase that company's services or products. An action is democracy in action, expecting officials to be servants of the people rather than to act as if they are the people's lords and masters.

ORGANIZING IN THE LOCAL CHURCH

Thus far we have examined the principles and strategies of community organizing for neighborhood and city transformation. However, organizing can also be used to transform the interior life of your congregation. The principles of organizing can be used to build a powerful relational congregation centered on glorifying God through working for the transformation of the world rather than through building programs.

Individual and house meetings throughout an entire congregation can be a central activity of both church elders and pastors, engaging members in conversations about those issues and concerns that really matter to them. Rather than building the church around committees to which members are reluctantly recruited, both the interior work and the mission outreach of the congregation can be built around action teams enabling members to address both community and church issues about which they really care. Hundreds of very successful churches have used organizing principles to recreate their institutions into powerful relational congregations and to make a profound difference in their neighborhoods.[5]

This chapter has explored the process for organizing for community or church action in the public arena. These are principles and strategies that work. But are they truly biblical? Nowhere in Scripture will we find a text that reads, "Thou shalt do community organizing." But the principles of community organizing are woven through the warp and woof of Scripture as it presents a theology of relational power. How else can we understand the intense encounters Jesus had with people like the Samaritan woman than as individual meetings—listening to their hearts, affirming and challenging them, and agitating them to think through their faith, beliefs and convictions? How else can we understand the investment of time Jesus made in his disciples than as an ongoing, traveling house meeting—reflecting with them, teaching them, calling them forth to become all he intended them to be? How else can we understand Nehemiah's meetings with King Artaxerxes, Asaph and Sanballat than as research actions? And how else can we understand Moses' confrontation of Pharaoh than as an action?

The Scriptures are replete with both the wise use of relational power and the abuse of unilateral power. If the church would allow Scripture to speak for itself, we would begin to discern the ministry to which God is calling us as he seeks to use us to work for the transformation of the public life of our communities, cities and nations. God has called us to work for the transformation of the world. But such transformation can occur only as we learn to use the relational power at our disposal.

9

BIBLICAL TACTICS FOR CHANGE
AVOIDED BY TODAY'S CHURCH

IN THIS CHAPTER WE WILL EXAMINE some essential tactics used in the Scriptures to enable God's people to act powerfully to change or influence the systems. However, there is something strange about each of these tactics: The church assiduously avoids them today! That these are biblical tactics is beyond any question. Why then does the church not use them?

AVOIDED BIBLICAL TACTICS

Accountability. Perhaps the classic case of demanding accountability from the powerful is the story of King David and Bathsheba. While his army is at war, David remains behind in Jerusalem. From the roof of his palace he sees a beautiful woman bathing. Her name is Bathsheba, the wife of Uriah, a leader in David's army. David brings Bathsheba to his home and has sex with her. She becomes pregnant. To cover up his wrongdoing, David calls Uriah home on the pretext of reporting to the king the progress of the war. His assumption is that Uriah will sleep with his wife and therefore David's immoral act will be covered over. However, Uriah refuses to go to his home. Frustrated, David compounds his crime by adding murder to it. He sends Uriah back to the front and commands Joab to place him in the most vulnerable part of the battlefield, where he is killed. David then marries Bathsheba. The king seems to have been successful in covering up his multiple crimes.

But he has reckoned without Nathan the prophet. Nathan comes to David and tells him a story about a rich man who took a poor man's only lamb. David said to Nathan, "As the LORD lives, the man who has done this deserves to die; he shall restore the lamb fourfold, because he did this thing, and because he had no pity." Nathan said to David, "You are the man!" (2 Sam 12:5-7).

What follows is a demand for accountability unparalleled in the Bible. Nathan is almost brutal in his confrontation of the king. He exposes the entirety of both David's lust and the deception and immorality of his treatment of Uriah. The prophet then lays out the inevitable consequences of David's compounded sin: "Thus says the LORD: I will raise up trouble against you from within your own house; and I will take your wives before your eyes, and give them to your neighbor, and he shall lie with your wives in the sight of this very sun. For you did it secretly; but I will do this thing before all Israel, and before the sun" (2 Sam 12:11-12).

David repents, and God forgives him. But God does not wipe out the consequences of David's sin. David's child born to the seduced Bathsheba dies, and the scourge of family unfaithfulness, sexual lust and lust for power that was launched by David's sin tears his household to pieces.

This is one of many biblical examples of leaders and ordinary people holding the powerful accountable—whether their power is political, economic or religious, whether they are heathen or believer, whether they are a leader of government, a spiritual leader, a disciple (Mk 8:31-33) or even a couple obsessed with their money (Acts 5:1-11). Yet the church avoids holding its people accountable today. I have often heard pastors say, "Why, I can't demand accountability of my church members for the sloppy job they do or for reneging on a commitment." Oh, yes you can! They may become angry, but they will respect you for it.

Confrontation. A second tactic used repeatedly by the biblical people of God to change the systems was that of confrontation. An excellent example of this is found in Acts 16:11-40. The apostle Paul and Silas are in Philippi, beginning the building of a church around the household of Lydia, a wealthy merchant. Each day Paul and Silas go to the town square to proclaim the gospel. On their way, they are accosted by a slave woman who can foretell the future and who is being exploited by her owners, who charge considerable sums for her to tell people's fortunes. On seeing Paul and Silas, this possessed woman follows them, crying, "These men are slaves of the Most High God, who proclaim to you a way of salvation." Paul finally becomes annoyed with her and says to her possessing spirit, "I order you in the name of Jesus Christ to come out of her" (Acts 16:17-18). And it does!

The owners, deprived of their source of income, are enraged and create a riot. They bring Paul and Silas to the Roman magistrates, who strip off their clothes, beat them and throw them in jail. In doing so, these magistrates have made a grave error. Paul is a Roman citizen, and Roman law provides him due process, protecting him from public humiliation, flogging and jail until the accusations made against him have been proven in a court of law. To guarantee that a Roman citizen's rights were not accidentally ignored, Roman law *required* that a magistrate ask *every* person accused of a crime whether or not he or she was a Roman citizen. But the magistrates assume Paul isn't a Roman citizen, and therefore they neglect to ask that legally required question.

Paul isn't going to let these magistrates get away with such a serious oversight. Thus his confrontation of them begins. Paul and Silas are placed into stocks "in the innermost cell" of the Philippi prison. There they pray and sing hymns. The jailer and the other prisoners listen to them, wondering what kind of mad men these are—and perhaps the jailer thinks, "How foolish these fellows are, praying to their God. Do they think that somehow their God will rescue them?"

God does rescue them! "Suddenly there was an earthquake, so violent that the foundations of the prison were shaken; and immediately all the doors were opened and everyone's chains were unfastened" (Acts 16:26). With the prison destroyed, the guard fears his prisoners have escaped. Roman law required execution for a guard who allowed his prisoners to escape. So the jailer draws his sword, intent on saving face by committing suicide. But Paul saves him, crying out, "Do not harm yourself, for we are all here" (Acts 16:28). The grateful guard brings Paul and Silas out of the prison, takes them to his home, bathes them and tends to their wounds.

Can you imagine the state of mind of this jailer? To say "his mind was blown" would be putting it mildly. In just a few minutes he went from scorn to incredulity to fear to the decision to kill himself to relief and gratitude. No wonder he asks Paul and Silas, "Sirs, what must I do to be saved?" So "he and his entire family were baptized without delay . . . [and] he had become a believer in God" (Acts 16:33-34).

Why is such attention paid to the jailer? One reason, of course, was to tell of his conversion. But the second reason was to explain what caused the jailer to move from being simply a jailer doing his job to becoming a most forceful advocate for Paul and Silas. The change of role of the jailer is the connecting link between the events of Acts 16:19-23 (before Paul and Silas are thrown into jail) and 16:35-40 (after Paul and Silas are released from jail).

The next day the magistrates send the police to the jailer to tell him to release Paul and Silas, who are now under house arrest in the jailer's home. The jailer comes to Paul, bearing the good news. He is not prepared for Paul's reply: "They have beaten us in public, uncondemned, *men who are Roman citizens,* and have thrown us in prison; and now are they going to discharge us in secret? Certainly not! Let them come and take us out themselves" (Acts 16:37, emphasis mine).

The jailer is stunned. He wasn't aware that Paul and Silas were Roman citizens. What a severe mistake the magistrates have made—a severe enough mistake that if Paul prosecutes them, they will lose their position and authority in the Roman Empire. Now thoroughly on Paul and Silas's side, the jailer tells the police the bad news, and they report it to the magistrates. So the magistrates come to the jailer's home and publicly apologize. Then they nicely ask the two to leave the city. Paul, in essence, says to the magistrates, "We'll leave when we get around to leaving." And in no hurry to leave, Paul and Silas go "to Lydia's home; and when they had seen and encouraged the brothers and sisters there, they departed" (Acts 16:38-40).

This is a story of in-your-face confrontation. It is a confrontation of the economic forces of Philippi who would seek to make profit off a possessed slave girl. It is a confrontation of the Philippi jailer and the laws of the state that would make him attempt suicide. But most of all, it is a confrontation of the magistrates of Philippi—the official representatives of the Roman Empire in that city. It is the public humiliation of these magistrates. It is an action that sends a message, loud and clear, to the Roman system throughout the world: "Don't mess with us Christians! We know the Roman law as well as you do. And we will use that law to its fullest extent to protect ourselves and to serve the cause of Christ. So be careful when you deal with Christians. Be very careful!" And that message wasn't lost on Rome, as Acts 21—28 clearly demonstrates.

As I look back over my life, I realize that each major growing time was initiated by someone confronting me. As the pastor under whom I worked as a seminary intern put it, "To get Linthicum to produce, I've learned you have to give him both a pat on the back and a kick in the rump!"

Civil disobedience. A third tactic presented in the Scripture is that of civil disobedience. One of the best such stories is found in Exodus 1:8-10, 15-20. The king of Egypt ordered the Hebrew midwives Shiphrah and Puah to kill Hebrew baby boys.

> But the midwives feared God; they did not do as the king of Egypt commanded them, but they let the boys live. So the king of Egypt summoned the midwives and said to them, "Why have you done this, and allowed the boys to live?" The midwives said to Pharaoh, "Because the Hebrew women are not like the Egyptian women; for they are vigorous and give birth before the midwife comes to them." So God dealt well with the midwives; and the people multiplied and became very strong. (Ex 1:17-20)

Because they "feared God," Shiphrah and Puah simply disobeyed Pharaoh. Told to kill the male babies, these midwives refused to do so. And then, when asked by Pharaoh why his plan was failing, they lied to him. Pharaoh accepted their explanation, and "the people multiplied and became very strong."

This is a classic case of civil disobedience. Shiphrah and Puah refused to follow the Pharaoh's orders and lied to cover up their defiance (they could not have openly defied the Pharaoh and lived). And God blessed their disobedience. Of course, this was only a temporary reprieve. Eventually, frustrated by the midwives, Pharaoh gave the order, "Every boy that is born to the Hebrews you shall throw into the Nile, but you shall let every girl live" (Ex 1:22). But Shiphrah and Puah had won a temporary reprieve that saved the lives of at least some Hebrew children.

Civil disobedience works best when those who are protesting are not politically powerful enough to successfully confront. Even though it is passively resistant, the power of civil disobedience is enormous. The witness to that was its use by Gandhi in eventually overthrowing the might of the British Empire in India—or even more clearly, its use by the civil rights movement as the means to win strategic political struggles in the South and to raise the consciousness of all the United States regarding our nationwide racism.

Negotiation. Negotiation is another tactic offered in Scripture to bring about change. One example of negotiation is found in Acts 15:1-29. The church was locked in a fierce debate. Christianity had begun as a Jewish sect, in which one had to be a Jew to become a Christian. But under the ministry of Paul and Barnabas, Gentiles were now converting to Christ. Could they do that? Could a Gentile actually become a Christian without converting to Judaism first? Did a Gentile have to first conform to Jewish law (and thus be circumcised and obey the law of Moses) before he or she could receive salvation through Christ? That was the issue with which the first Jerusalem council had to deal.

Both sides gather—the Judaizers, and Paul and Barnabas—along with the fathers of the church, including Peter and James the brother of Jesus. Those who defend the Jewish grounding of the Christian sect first argue their case. Paul and Barnabas present their argument that Gentiles don't need to become Jews in order to become Christians—in essence, making Christianity into its own religion distinct from Judaism. Peter speaks to the question, taking the side of Paul and Barnabas. Finally "after there had been much debate," the church fathers consult and James then speaks for them: "I have reached the decision that we should not trouble those Gentiles who are turning to God, but we should write to them to abstain only from things polluted by idols and from fornication and from whatever has been strangled and from blood. For in every city, for generations past, Moses has had those who proclaim him, for he has been read aloud every sabbath in the synagogues" (Acts 15:19-21).

This is a clear example of working out a negotiated settlement. In essence Paul and Barnabas won. A Gentile could become a Christian without becoming a Jew first. Therefore that Gentile need not submit to the ritual of circumcision nor would he or she be expected to obey the law of Moses as a precondition for salvation. Only receiving Christ as one's Savior and Lord was necessary for salvation.

But although that might be true, a Gentile shouldn't become an offense to a Jewish Christian, the church fathers adjudicated. Although a Gentile is under grace and not under the law, he or she should be careful to observe those Jewish laws that would most bring offense to Jews if they were flagrantly ignored. Therefore the Gentiles were told, don't eat meat that has been sacrificed to pagan idols. Don't follow sexual practices that are offensive to Jews. When with Jews, don't eat meat that is not kosher. Be sensitive to your brother and sister Jewish Christians and treat them with love and kindness.

This is a negotiated settlement. Each side has to give up something to be at peace with those Christians with whom they radically disagree. The Judaizers have to abandon their position that Gentiles have to live under the law before they can live under grace. Gentiles have to seek to understand the Judaizers and to observe the law when in their presence. Both sides are not to give offense to the other.

I once asked a church historian what was the main lesson he had learned from church history. His response was, "The history of Christianity has been one sorry story of Christians making their last-ditch stands in the wrong ditches!" In other words, Christians tend to fight over issues that seem to be terribly important at the time but are not as systemic to the faith as we might think they are. An important biblical strategy that we would do well to follow is to learn how to negotiate even on those issues most important to us.

Agitation. A final biblical tactic the church avoids today is agitation. Perhaps the person who most practiced the tactic of agitation in the Bible was Jesus. In all four Gospels he is described as a person who presses others, either to call forth the best in them or to call them to accountability. One such story of agitation is Jesus' encounter with Peter before his death, as recorded in Matthew 26:31-35.

Here Jesus tells the disciples that once he is arrested and placed on trial all of them will desert him. Peter responds, "Though all become deserters because of you, I will never desert you." Jesus replies, "Truly I tell you, this very night, before the cock crows, you will deny me three times." Peter retorts, "Even though I must die with you, I will not deny you" (Mt 26:33-35).

This story is followed by Jesus' arrest, imprisonment and trial before the high priest. Peter follows Jesus to the courtyard of the high priest's palace where he encounters people who expose him for who he is—a follower of Jesus. Three times he denies even knowing Jesus (much less following him). The cock crows, reminding Peter of Jesus' words. And Matthew concludes, "And [Peter] went out and wept bitterly" (Mt 26:75).

This is a perfect example of Jesus agitating Peter. His original statement, "You will all become deserters," was an effort to agitate all the disciples. But it was Peter who took the bait and responded with conviction that he would never deny Jesus. Jesus agitated him further, indicating exactly how and when Peter would deny him. But even then Peter remained firm in his protestation.

In reality, not only Jesus agitated Peter. So did the servant girl who accused him, "You also were with Jesus the Galilean," as well as a second servant girl, who declared, "This man was with Jesus of Nazareth." Finally a number of bystanders asserted, "Certainly you are also one of them, for your accent betrays you" (Mt 26:69, 71, 73).

Why is it important for Peter to be so agitated? And why would Jesus agitate him at this most vulnerable moment of Peter's life? This is one of the two last opportunities Jesus has to prepare Peter for leadership of the church. In this incident he must make Peter aware of his very real weakness and capacity to sin—for it is clear from the Scripture that Peter thinks more highly of himself than he ought to think. Jesus must also communicate to Peter his forgiveness of him, which he does in an ensuing story of his restoration of Peter in John 21:15-19. Jesus' desire is not to annoy or irritate Peter; it is to call him to accountability. And this he succeeds in doing by agitating him that night.

Accountability, confrontation, civil disobedience, negotiation, agitation—all are biblical tactics to bring about change in people and in institutions. All are tactics the church tends to avoid today. But we must ask of these tactics, "Which proved truly effective, and which did not?" The answer is that all were effective. Each tactic was effective within its particular context.

Each tactic also brought about the desired change. Nathan got David to repent and admit his guilt. Paul brought the Roman magistrates to their knees, begging his pardon. Shiphrah and Puah saved Israelite male babies from death. Paul and Silas got the church to endorse Gentile conversions as authentic. Jesus helped prepare Peter for church leadership by getting him to know himself. Each tactic was successful in bringing about change in the political, economic or religious system or person with which it was dealing.

These tactics are effective and capable of bringing about change when used in the appropriate environment. For example, if Shiphrah and Puah had tried to use the tactic of confrontation on Pharaoh, it would have failed because they lacked the capacity to confront. Or if Nathan had used the tactic of civil disobedience on David rather than calling him to accountability, David likely would have interpreted his action as defiance of the crown. That was because Nathan needed to directly confront David and not appear simply to be resistant. Each person in question chose the appropriate tactic for the context in which it was to be used. Each ascertained the appropriate means to exercise power in the situation and, consequently, got the result he or she was expecting.

Any and all of these tactics, when used by God's people, are capable of bringing about substantive change in a city and its systems—even when those systems are acting out of values other than the building of a shalom community. Each tactic can be part of the tool kit of Christian leaders who want to work for change in their church, community, city or nation. And we should not dismiss such tactics as being inappropriate for Christians to use, because if such tactics are good enough for Jesus, Paul, Barnabas, Nathan, and Shiphrah and Puah, they ought to be good enough for us!

JESUS ON CONFRONTATION

If we as the church are to work for shalom community in the world as it is today, we will have to be willing to confront the systems and powers. But of the biblical tactics with which we have just worked—accountability, confrontation, civil disobedience, negotiation and agitation—the tactic with which Christians have the greatest trouble is confrontation. Yet of all the tactics it is perhaps the most pivotal and strategic. I believe that the best person in the Scriptures to help us use confrontation is our Lord and Savior, Jesus Christ.

Confrontation is an integral part of any empowering process for a community, a city or even a church. Christians have trouble with it because we believe it to be inconsistent with a loving, Christlike faith. But confrontation is the healthy process that enables humans to resolve pronounced differences of opinion. You can't hope to bring about significant change—in a church or in a Christian organization or in the world—and avoid confrontation.

One of the difficulties we have with confrontation is that it seems so violent. But in reality, confrontation and violence are opposites. Confrontation is the face-to-face, direct encounter between people seeking resolution. It is vigorous negotiation. But the purpose of confrontation is not a ventilation of one's hostilities but the resolution of the differences between people and groups. The word *confrontation* literally means "at foreheads" (*con*—"at" or "with"; *front*—"forehead"), so named by the ancients because when we confront we get "in each other's face."

Violence, on the other hand, is the exercise of physical force in order to gain one's own way. The objective of confrontation is resolution; the objective of violence is to win. Whether it is a person or a government that is acting violently, the purpose of violence is to defeat the opposition, not to come to a negotiated settlement. In a profound sense, violence is often an indication that confrontation has failed. People resort to violence when their efforts to confront a system have met—not with the decision of the system to negotiate—but with the system either stonewalling or acting violently itself.

One of the most confrontational people in the Bible was Jesus. How confrontational was he? Well, simply consider the number of incidents in the ministry of Jesus that appear in just one of the Gospels—Luke. There are 133 stories or incidents recorded in Luke in which the adult Jesus figures. Of those 133 stories, 116 are confrontational in nature. The remainders are primarily miracles or commentary (for example, Jesus went from point A to point B).

Of the 116 incidents in which Jesus was confrontational, 66 were confrontations of representatives of the religious, political or economic systems of either Israel or Rome, 45 were confrontations by Jesus of his disciples or followers and 10 were confrontations of demons. One would have expected Jesus to confront the systems and demons. But given the significant number of confrontations by Jesus of his disciples and friends, one would have to say that Jesus was an equal opportunity agitator.

Only one action by Jesus in Luke was violent. That was the cleansing of the temple when he "began to drive out those who were selling things there" (Lk 19:45-48). One can argue that it was the cleansing of the temple—that single resort to physical violence on Jesus' part—that got Jesus killed, and not his many confrontations of the leaders of Israel. His confrontations made the leaders exceedingly angry, but their decision to get Jesus crucified was not made until *after* his cleansing of the temple (Lk 20:20; 22:1-6). Violence begot violence—and that was Jesus' intention.

The inevitable question we must ask about Jesus' confrontational ministry is, What is at the heart of such confrontation? What was driving Jesus to confront friend and foe alike? That question is perhaps most profoundly answered in Matthew 23, the story of Jesus' final confrontation of the Pharisees. Throughout his ministry, Jesus has been calling on these religious leaders to see how they've misused the law by building up the power and wealth of the Jewish elite of which they were part, while covering it all with a pious veneer. He had repeatedly called upon them to embrace the full jubilee, to redistribute wealth so that poverty would be eliminated and to proclaim both spiritual and physical liberty throughout the land. But they had refused, preferring to maintain themselves in positions of power and wealth rather than to seek the shalom of their people. Now their resistance to his message has built to a crescendo, and Jesus bursts forth in what can only be called a diatribe against them. (Read Matthew 23:1-39 out loud and with conviction, and you will realize that Jesus was certainly not being "nice.")

His final attack begins with these biting words: "The scribes and the Pharisees sit on Moses' seat; therefore, do whatever they teach you and follow it; *but do not do as they do,* for they do not practice what they teach" (Mt 23:2-3, emphasis mine). That sets the theme for the remainder of the attack, as Jesus proclaims seven "woes" against these religious leaders. But Jesus' intention in confronting the Pharisees comes out most clearly and poignantly in the closing lines of his argument against them: "You snakes, you brood of vipers! How can you escape being sentenced to hell? . . . Jerusalem, Jerusalem, the city that kills the prophets and stones those who are sent to it! How often have I desired to gather your children together as a hen gathers her brood under her wings, and you were not willing! See, your house is left to you, desolate" (Mt 23:33, 37-39).

Remember that the Latin root for the English word *anger* is the word *grief.* What was at the heart of Jesus' grief and anger? Jesus confronted the religious leaders of Israel (the Pharisees and scribes), the economic system of Israel (the Sadducees, priests, high priests and Jerusalem religious aristocracy) and the political system (Pilate representing Rome; the high priest and Herod

Antipas representing the local political order). He confronted them because they were the enemies of the people and were committed to building their own power rather than building the shalom community of Israel.

Jesus also confronted inside the community of faith. He confronted the disciples in order to prepare them for leadership of the church and for ministry with the poor and powerless, and to enable them to understand and articulate the values and vision of the shalom community. The only people Jesus rarely confronted were the poor, marginalized or weak. They already had enough dumped on them.

What drove Jesus to so relentlessly confront friend and foe alike? It was love. Jesus confronted out of love for those powerful Pharisees and scribes who could not see that their policies of greed and lust for power would bring about the destruction of their nation. He confronted out of love for the people who would eventually become the victims of the system's lust for unilateral power that would lead to the destruction of Jerusalem. He confronted out of love for his disciples, who were responsible for building the vision of the shalom community, the kingdom of God, out of the destruction those Pharisees and scribes would bring upon their people.

Because he loved the people and his disciples and the nation's leaders so much, Jesus was agitational. He was seeking to agitate because only out of extreme discomfort and agitation would (1) people be sufficiently motivated to change and (2) systems be forced to change or face themselves. The first did happen to some degree—some people profoundly changed and became the rock upon which Christ would build his church, seeking the transformation of Roman and Jewish society. Other people didn't change at all and missed the greatest revolution in human history. The systems would not change at all; they would not face themselves, but blindly sped on in their greed and lust for unilateral power—and their destruction at the hands of Rome became inevitable. And therefore Jesus wept over the city.

As we reflect on the confrontational ministry of Jesus, we see crucial elements of good confrontation that we need to follow both in dealing with the systems and with the church.

- Let the people, along with their leaders (in some cases), determine that confrontation must occur.

173

- Separate the confronted person from the issue, if possible (not so much "you are bad" as "what you are doing is wrong").

- Personalize your confrontation of the systems. Don't simply confront the system (or even a department or division of the system), but rather specific individuals who hold the power to effect the changes you want made. (Remember that the person you select to confront is your "target," not your enemy.)

- Research the situation and the target, learning the target's strengths and weaknesses.

- Create a plan for confronting the target.

- Demand accountability from the target by meeting with him or her (or requesting a meeting) to enter into good-faith negotiations.

- If the target refuses to meet, or meets but does not enter into good-faith negotiations, those doing the confrontation must confront the target publicly. Any such meeting will place a clear demand before the target ("Will you or won't you?").

- Continue such a strategy until you reach a resolution agreeable to both parties. Then celebrate with the body and evaluate its action.

- If the struggle between the confronters and the target has proven particularly bitter, but you have come to an agreement acceptable to both parties in the conflict, find ways afterward to rebuild relationships between the target and yourself. No target should be permitted to remain a permanent enemy.

ORGANIZING PEOPLE FOR POWER

Through this and the two previous chapters, I have attempted to present principles for the *practice* of relational power, using the Bible as our main textbook on both understanding power and learning how to use it for Christ and his kingdom. But does this work? Does the use of relational power bring about the transformation both of people and of their communities? Let me share with you the story of a ministry in which I had the privilege to play a small part.

In 1987 I received a telephone call from Saeed Rallia-Ram, the executive director of World Vision India (WV India). "Come on over and help us," Saeed said to me. I had been heading World Vision's Office of Urban Advance for eighteen months, introducing that Christian relief and development organization to the principles and strategies of community organizing. Saeed explained to me that WV India had made the decision to significantly increase its work among the poor in the major cities of India, and they needed help in developing an effort that would move beyond relief and social services to the empowerment of people—primarily those of the lowest caste.

Soon I arrived in Madras,[1] India's fourth-largest city, the location of WV India's offices. There I began meeting with its senior staff to plan together the strategy this relief and development agency wanted to pursue in the cities of the world's most populous subcontinent. My work with WV India, which would continue over the next ten years, was similar to the services any community organizing network provides its on-the-ground organizations. I helped plan strategy, train organizers, supervise staff, participate in evaluation and lead three- to ten-day training events for key community leaders, organizers, volunteers and religious leaders. But it was the work the local organizers and community leaders did that truly built this remarkable "people of power."

The organizing effort that WV India initiated was named Organizing People for Progress (OPP). It has been focused for its entirety among the poorest of the poor in India's cities, especially the Untouchables. The Untouchables, or Dalits, number more than 300 million and are born at the bottom of Hinduism's caste system. As their name implies, they are considered by many other Hindus to be "untouchable," uneducated and impoverished people who are to be avoided. Since the ending of the British Raj, a few Dalits have achieved political power and from time to time have shown themselves capable of organizing considerable short-term power. But they have not been able to build permanent power organizations that would free them from impoverishment and ignorance.

Organizing People for Progress began in 1988 in five of the worst slums and squatter settlements in Madras. By 1994 it had expanded to slums of four cities in southwest and southeast India. Today OPP is at work in the slums of the thirteen largest cities of India. Let's look at one example of this work.

In July 1990 the Slum Clearance Board of the city of Madras made the decision to rid that city of the Untouchables who made their homes on the streets. Overnight six thousand street-dwellers were rounded up and their makeshift homes bulldozed. They were tossed into the back of army trucks and driven to Vellachery, an almost inaccessible floodplain on the outskirts of Madras. There all six thousand of them were unceremoniously dumped on the ground and told to fend for themselves. No housing or infrastructure of any kind was provided.

Vellachery was a terrible place in which to be abandoned—an immense floodplain, separated from the Bay of Bengal by a narrow ridge of sand. Twice each year, monsoons flooded Vellachery with salt water. Because of those floods, nothing grew—no plants, no trees, no crops. No human being had ever lived there. Further, because it was unpopulated, there were no roads and no public transportation from Madras into Vellachery—no way to reach the outside world and no way for the outside world to reach it except by a four-wheel-drive vehicle.

WV India heard what had happened to Madras's street people and sent Rajkumar, its lead organizer, to investigate. Rajkumar began visiting the people abandoned in Vellachery. Obviously their immediate need was simply to survive, so he instructed World Vision to bring in emergency aid. Soon the people were living in temporary tents, were being fed emergency rations and were receiving emergency health care.

Rajkumar continued to visit with the residents of Vellachery, listening to their stories, hearing their groans and their hopes, and building relationships with them. Soon he identified potential leaders, particularly among the women. He began house meetings with them, bringing in women organizers to work with them.

The women organizers asked all the women of Vellachery what they considered their most pressing problem. Together they agreed it was housing. They and their families needed to have permanent homes before the construction of a true community could begin. But housing is expensive and time-consuming to build. How was sufficient housing to be constructed to adequately house Vellachery's six thousand?

In their meetings, the women clearly analyzed the situation. It was the government that had created the problem by abandoning them in Vellachery. Therefore the government should solve the problem. The organizers asked the women if they would be willing to confront the government to make them build the housing. They indicated they would. Rajkumar took them to another slum where OPP had been organizing so they could meet with its people and observe how they were generating people power. So the organizers and women worked together to create a campaign that would get them their homes.

Over the next eighteen months the organized women and youth of Vellachery met with the appropriate government officials of both city and state, exerting intense pressure in creative ways. For example, to gain the co-operation of one government official, they occupied his suite of offices with an increasing number of women—eventually more than five hundred—and refused to leave until he negotiated with them. By such tactics they won concession after concession. Finally after eighteen months they had built enough power and credibility that they met with the prime minister of the State of Tamil Nadu (comparable to a governor of an American state) and gained from her the final written order for the housing to be built.

The State of Tamil Nadu built close to three thousand homes for all the families living in Vellachery at that time, so that everyone got a home. The land upon which each house was built was deeded by the city to each family, and the homes were sold to the families for thirty dollars apiece (payable over a three-year period). In this way, each of these Untouchables became legal homeowners for the first time in their lives.

But there was more! Over the next six years, beginning in 1990, a new community was created. The people developed their own "city" plan. Having established themselves as a powerful force in Madras, the organized community was able to meet with public, private and nonprofit decision makers with relative ease. The women organized to get the state to build a mammoth flood-retention wall so that Vellachery would never be flooded again. The city of Madras installed streetlights, plumbing, sewers, toilets and running water in each home (an unheard-of luxury for India's poor). The men's association got the city to build a road from Madras to Vellachery, to pave the interior streets of the community, to haul in earth, to plant trees and to build several playgrounds for children. The youth association negotiated with the Madras school system to build a school and a library. The city built community and health centers, and the youth successfully negotiated with nongovernmental organizations other than World Vision to provide books for the library, supplies for the school and funds for staff positions in all four institutions. Finally, the people successfully organized to get the transportation authority to run bus lines to Vellachery so the people could have access to the city, its jobs and its commerce.

With the growing transformation of Vellachery, it was inevitable that other Untouchable families would move there. Therefore the people organized to keep the government steadily building homes in the community. The homes now exceed seven thousand, with more than twenty thousand residents, still following the principle of one home for each family.

The people elected their own leaders to administer their community. They employed men and women from their midst to run the library, the health center and the community center. With the guidance of WV India, the people formed several business cooperatives that employed the people of Vellachery and provided a steady income stream to that community.

A profound spiritual renewal also occurred in Vellachery over the years of this organizing effort. Of course, energy and optimism was created as the people experienced victory after victory and as they worked at building a town together. But there was significant faith sharing as well. Vellachery is about 90 percent Hindu, 8 percent Muslim and 2 percent Christian; that reality is potentially divisive. The organizers worked at overcoming this religious division by getting the residents who were involved in the associations (action teams) to identify the values they wanted for their community. They studied each other's holy books to better understand and embrace these common values. That gave people permission to talk freely about religious commonalities and differences, and fostered a growing respect for each other. It also increased opportunities for considerable faith sharing, especially by the Christians, about whose beliefs the others proved very curious. (This process of faith sharing will be explored more fully in chapter ten.)

Organizing People for Progress successfully trains the poor to empower themselves through collective action. Organized slum areas in thirteen Indian cities now practice participatory democracy and meet with and apply pressure to urban power structures. People develop their capacity to lead.

The result is social, structural and spiritual transformation of the Untouchables into a people of power.[2]

Just before I left World Vision in 1995, I returned to Madras and was privileged to be asked by its residents to visit Vellachery. There I toured the rapidly transforming slum and met with the leadership team of the women's association. I asked them how they felt about Vellachery when they first came there. I heard words like *angry, upset, afraid, betrayed.* Then I asked them how they felt now. Responses demonstrating pride, power, joy and hopefulness filled the room. But I will never forget in particular what one woman said: "When I lived on the streets, my soul was very unhappy; it was restless; it had no place to sleep. But now that I live in Vellachery, my soul is quiet within me because it has now found a home where it can be with God."

10

THE SPIRITUALITY
OF RELATIONAL POWER

IF ONE IS TO BE SERIOUS ABOUT building power in a church or community, then he or she must work to achieve three primary objectives:

1. Seek to *build the relational power* of the people through their capacity to bring change to their situation (especially in their capacity to negotiate powerfully with the systems).

2. Discover, call forth and *build leadership* among the people.

3. *Create community* across church and organizational lines through the articulation and embracing of common values and a common spirituality.

Thus far in part two of this book we have worked exclusively with the first objective: building the relational power of the people. On the whole, the church has done a commendable job of building leadership down through the centuries, so we won't dwell on this objective here.[1] In this chapter, we will concentrate on the third primary objective for building power: creating community around values.

THE CREATION OF COMMUNITY
The third objective of community organizing is the building of community around the exercise of relational power. That exercise is essentially a spiritual

one. Therefore it is important to conclude our reflection together with how exercising relational power can build spirituality. Community is built through articulating values, sharing faith and embracing relational spirituality.[2]

Articulating the values of relational power. One of the best ways to create relational power is to identify, own and articulate the common values that bind people together in a relational culture. There is great potential in spending time fostering a relationship with others through individual and house meetings and through working together in research actions and in actions. This work of getting to know the convictions and beliefs of another person and building trust and confidence in each other by working together creates a unique bond. That bond is one of discovering, articulating and owning the values you hold in common.

What are those values upon which relational power is built? Chief among them is a common commitment to building a relational culture where relational power is exercised. To exercise relational power, we must believe that power is found in relationships. Rather than defining power as solely unilateral, we intentionally exercise power relationally by holding individual and house meetings, and by participating in research actions and actions together, seeking to change the directions and priorities of unilateral institutions. Even if we are not convinced of the effectiveness of relational power, by exercising that power together we are acting our way into a new way of thinking.

This, of course, is exactly how human beings learn. We don't learn how to ride a bicycle by attending a Bicycling 101 class; we gain a skill by *doing* it and then evaluating, and doing it again and evaluating once again—usually with someone mentoring us who helps us improve—until it becomes an accomplished skill. We don't think our way into a new way of acting; rather we act our way into a new way of thinking. And that is precisely what happens when we exercise the strategies and tactics of relational power. We discover that it truly is very powerful. And so we embrace being in relationship with other people in a new way, with increasing skill and with increasing dedication.

The process through which we move in embracing the values of a relational culture is that of discovering, articulating and owning those values. Initially we discover them. Someone has an individual meeting with us and perhaps calls on us again. We are invited to a house meeting, and we attend.

Gradually we get increasingly involved in this organizing effort. Involvement in a house meeting helps us identify the area of public concern we care the most about, and we get involved in an action team around that concern. There two things happen. We become involved in working with others to plan and to implement research actions and actions and to evaluate our actions (and thus hone our skill). And we begin conducting individual meetings ourselves and sharing in the leadership of house meetings. The student has become the professor. The "mentee" has become the mentor.

As we move through this process of increasing participation, we find ourselves acting our way into a new way of thinking. Conducting individual meetings ourselves, providing leadership to house meetings and becoming involved in action teams leads to an increased commitment to and ownership of the exercise of relational power. And the more our commitment to relational power increases, the more we start to articulate it. Our involvement in and exercise of relational power has caused us to begin thinking about how effective we can actually be by exercising relational power publicly. And so we become increasingly adept at articulating this newfound power. We have become disciples of the power of a relational culture.

People involved in the exercise of relational power value that power—and therefore they value a relational culture. We humans are made to be in relationship with each other, and our hearts will be restless until we find such relationship with each other. And for those who are "children of Abraham" (Muslims, Jews and Christians), such a relational culture is made perfect in our mutual relationships with God. Consequently, those engaged in the exercise of relational power work in their local situation to build a culture of relational power among and within the relational institutions (churches, religious communities, clubs, parent-teacher groups, mission agencies, people's organizations) so they can engage the public and private unilateral institutions of their community to adopt policies and practices that place people as their primary concern.

Those who exercise relational power also hold justice as a primary value. Precisely because we are committed to a relational culture, we are committed to a just culture. And that means opposition to any effort of any unilateral political, economic, educational or cultural institution that would act out of a lust for dominance or favoritism. Those committed to the exercise of relational power are going to be opposed to the oppressive policies and actions of any institution. Consequently, those engaged in the exercise of relational power work in their local situation to demand justice from any such institution and to powerfully negotiate so that such justice will be carried out.

In addition to valuing relational culture and justice, the organizing community embraces a commitment to the reduction, and even elimination, of poverty. In a world where there is a sufficiency for all, the hoarding of the world's resources by any nation, economy, business or class so that they have abundance at the expense of others is unacceptable. For example, enough grain is produced throughout the world in a year to provide every human being with 3,600 calories per day. However, one-quarter of the world is starving while North America and Western Europe consume 70 percent of the world's grain—much of which goes to feeding cattle and brewing booze.[3] Therefore those practicing a relational culture would be committed to a stewardship of the common wealth of the world so that no one is in need. Consequently those engaged in the exercise of relational power work in their local situation to "maintain the rights of the poor and oppressed" by working for economic justice (Psalm 82:3 NIV).

A final common value would be a shared commitment to the Iron Rule: "Never do for others what they can do for themselves." This commitment recognizes that each of us as individuals and all of us as a relational culture are to assume responsibility for the practice of relational power, justice and an economics of sufficiency rather than of greed in our personal lives and our public actions.

These are the common values of a relational culture that we discover in exercising relational power together and that we own and articulate. For those who are "children of Abraham," there should be a particular affinity toward these values because they are so central to our respective religious traditions and our holy books (the Koran, the Hebrew Bible and the New Testament). It is hard to see how we could reject these values and still remain Christian, because this is so clearly what Christ was about and what God's intentions for human society are.

However, any human society is made up of people holding to many values and traditions—both religious and secular. How then can a commitment to common values knit us together into a relational culture in spite of our faith distinctives (including no faith at all)?

One of our organizing efforts in Chennai (Madras) is a great example of how a collection of people can be molded into an authentic community through relational values that they discover, articulate and own together. The Shastri Nagar organizing effort took place in one of the worst inner-city slums of Chennai. The center of the organizing effort was the women of that slum (the men proved to be too whipped by life to be "organizable"). Like most Indian communities, Shastri Nagar was religiously divided—consisting of Hindus (the majority), Muslims, Christians and secularists.

The women had successfully organized the slum to get government action on a number of infrastructure issues, such as replacing the three toilets for the five thousand residents with an adequate latrine system, installing streetlights and bringing electricity into the people's huts, and replacing muddy streets with asphalt roads. But now the problems with which the women's association began to deal were more substantive, having to do with the quality of their lives. To deal with these issues, there had to be some common convictions of what that community ought to be like. How would an organizer ever get Hindus, Muslims, Christians and secularists to embrace common values?

The organizer brought them to commonality around their twice-monthly meetings. At one of these meetings, she asked each woman to reflect over the next two weeks on naming the value around which each wanted to build the life of her community and then to return to the next meeting with her answer. They did this, and they discovered that the overwhelming value around which they wanted to build their community was sobriety.

"Why sobriety?" the organizer asked them. The women shared that their husbands, who worked as rickshaw drivers, day laborers or at other menial jobs, would be paid daily. Many of them would spend most of these daily wages on alcohol before ever getting home. They would arrive home drunk and aggressive. The result was that many of the wives were being beaten and abused. Therefore they longed for the virtue of sobriety.

After spending some time sharing their mutual stories of spousal abuse and drunkenness, the women were led by the organizer to discuss what they wanted to do about it. They decided on two parallel actions against their drunken spouses. The first was to be held on an upcoming national holiday. The women got their children to make placards, and then on that holiday (when their fathers would be home) the children staged a parade through the slum, calling for sobriety and displaying signs that had slogans like "Fathers, stop beating our mothers" and "Fathers, stop drinking." They particularly singled out the houses of the worst offenders for parading and shouting their slogans.

The other action was more substantive and ongoing. The women formed an intervention team. Then whenever a man would come home drunk, a signal would be sounded throughout Shastri Nagar, and the women would descend upon that man's home, pin him against the wall and shout at him to stop drinking until he would sink exhausted to the ground. Besieged, embarrassed and overwhelmed, the men stopped coming home drunk, and sobriety became the accepted behavior in the slum.

Because of the religious diversity of Shastri Nagar, peace was maintained simply by not talking about religion. Therefore it was never appropriate to speak about one's faith. In the twice-monthly meetings of the women's association, the organizer allotted time for reflection on how the intervention campaign was progressing. They reported with great glee how the drinking and drunkenness had almost stopped throughout the slum. Then the organizer did an almost unthinkable thing. She asked the women to be prepared to share at the next meeting how their respective religions and holy teachings taught the value of sobriety.

The next meeting came with great anticipation and was fully attended. Women shared with each other for the first time from their religious traditions about the value their religion placed upon sobriety. It was as if the lid had blown off; for the first time, these slum residents had been given permission to talk openly about their own and each other's religions—and talk they did! Someone suggested they needed to read their sacred texts on sobriety. And soon the ladies were caught up in studying the Bible and other sacred literature together. Thus it became acceptable in Shastri Nagar to talk about faith.

But words without action are meaningless, so the women decided that they would celebrate together selected "holy days" of each tradition in their slum. Rather than ignoring religious observances, the women's association concluded that there would be value in sharing in the celebration of such holy days. The holy days selected were the ones acceptable to those who were not of that tradition. Thus national holidays celebrating former outstanding Indian leaders were mutually observed. Two Christian holidays were chosen in which the whole community shared: Christmas and Easter. Why Christmas and Easter? Christmas was well known throughout India, and people liked the idea of celebrating the birth of a peasant child in a stable who grew up to become the Savior of his people. The celebration of the resurrection of Jesus was agreeable because Muslims believe in his resurrection and Hindus consider Jesus a god.

By following this strategy, the community was able to discover, articulate and own common values that helped build them into a truly relational community. And they began the process of sharing faith with each other.

Faith sharing. People in Faith United (PIFU) is a church-based community organization on the east side of Detroit. It is in one of the poorest neighborhoods of Detroit, where, twenty years ago, there was over 76 percent unemployment and only 2 percent of homes were owner occupied. When I was providing leadership to PIFU from 1979 through 1985, it consisted of thirteen churches, several community groups and a large number of community residents. Because of this mixture of active participants, the organization was not solely Christian. I participated both as an organizer and as the pastor of a church in a nearby community.

As a Christian I have always been concerned about sharing my faith. People would expect me to share that faith in "appropriate" settings, such as worship services, funerals or counseling situations. But I soon discovered that when I shared my faith in settings where one would not reasonably expect the preacher to share (a barber shop, a community committee meeting, a social gathering), people's eyes glazed over as they patiently waited for me to finish my "preacher thing."

Then one day it dawned on me. It takes two people to do the work of evangelism. It takes one person to share the gospel, but it takes another person to *hear* that gospel! I had placed all my emphasis on how I could more effectively share the good news. But I never thought about what I should do to motivate a person to *want to hear* that good news.

As I reflected on that insight, I asked myself what would cause a person to want to listen. And I decided it would have to be trust. What causes me to listen seriously to another person is that I take that person seriously—I trust what he or she has to say. I will listen to a medical doctor telling me what I should do to treat my health problem far more than I will listen to a layperson. Why? Simply because I trust the doctor's level of expertise. So a person will listen to you sharing your faith if they have a relationship with you that causes them to trust you. I found, therefore, that the sharing of my faith could most effectively occur in those relationships where I had really connected with people around commonly identified issues and in which we had built, owned and articulated common relational values together.

I had the opportunity to practice my newfound insight with Martin, one of the neighborhood participants in PIFU. Martin was a young African American living in that poor community who was attracted to our organizing effort. His life had little meaning before participation in PIFU. He was a fairly typical young adult without much purpose or direction, with a limited education and with a fair share of trouble with the authorities while growing up. He came into our organizing effort because I held an individual meeting with him and then invited him to a house meeting. For the first time, Martin began to believe he could have some measure of influence over the shaping of his own destiny. He found that organizing effort lifegiving; it gave him purpose and direction. He became increasingly involved and active in it.

I began to realize that Martin had solid leadership potential, even though he was only in his twenties, so I began to mentor him. He and I spent a great amount of time together, sharing in the planning of actions and research actions, standing side by side in confrontations, eating meals together, reflecting on the effectiveness of his leadership, and consuming vast amounts of coffee in restaurants as we would evaluate actions. The issues and concerns of Martin's life became very important to me, and mine to him, as our relationship grew and our bonds strengthened—even though we were separated by twenty-five years of age, different skin colors, different educational levels and different cultures.

One night, when we were debriefing a meeting together over coffee, Martin asked me, "Bob, why do you do this work?"

"What do you mean, Martin?" I responded.

"Well, you're a preacher, aren't you?"

"Sure."

"Then why do you take such an interest in me? You could be just like any other preacher, studying in your office, preaching on Sundays, minding your church. And instead, you spend all kinds of time with me and lots of other people like me. Why do you do it? Why do you care?"

So it was that I shared with Martin about Someone who cared enough about me to give his life for me and to rise again that I might have new life. And Martin listened intently as I shared my own testimony. As a result he asked me if he could receive this same Christ, "because if he means so much to you, I know he'll mean as much to me!"

Because of the relationship of trust and respect I had built with Martin, he asked me to share my faith. What an opportunity! I wasn't trying to "sell Jesus" to him. He wanted to know about Christ, and he wanted to know because of the relationship I had fostered with him. He had become a person who *wanted to hear* the gospel.

Involvement in empowerment ministries provides three foundations for sharing faith: the opportunity to build significant relationships with people based on individual and house meetings; the common ground of shared victories and defeats as you learn to exercise relational power together through actions and research actions; the identification, ownership and articulation of common values of a just, equitable and relational culture forged in living out the Iron Rule together. Those three foundations create a base upon which faith can be powerfully shared with people who are wide open to it being shared.

This is what eventually transpired in the organizing in Shastri Nagar. Out of the building of a relational culture, the success of common victories and the articulation of values an atmosphere conducive to faith sharing was created. Both the organizers and the Christian residents of Shastri Nagar did the sharing.

Faith sharing by the organizers occurred in a context none of them anticipated would be an avenue for such sharing. The open faith atmosphere in Shastri Nagar and the capacity of the women to organize around common values allowed many of the women to come to the female organizers with their personal problems. Soon organizers were spending considerable time listening to the personal concerns of women, encouraging them and, when appropriate, sharing Christ with them. The result was a number of women making decisions to receive Christ as their Savior.

This growing trend provided the opportunity for the organizers to bring together a newly converted woman with other Christian women from Shastri Nagar. They would hold "Christian house meetings" together to support and encourage each other. That in turn emboldened some of the women to share their faith with others. This new openness then led to a wider sharing of faith with young men and community leaders. The result was the formation of a small house church within that slum, as Christ became increasingly alive to the people there. But all this occurred because, as one person put it, "you don't have to put another religion down to put Christianity up." Rather, by creating an open faith-sharing atmosphere based on the claiming of common values, God could work through the relationships already built, and people would naturally come to Christ.

THE SPIRITUALITY OF RELATIONAL POWER

As Christians we proclaim that the crucifixion of Jesus was the act that purchased both our personal redemption and the corporate transformation of the world. But it is important for us to remember that Christian faith does not end with death on a cross, but with an empty tomb. With Christians down through the ages, we proclaim, "Christ is risen. He is risen indeed!" That resurrection is not just for us personally, but for the whole world. The apostle Paul wrote,

> I consider that the sufferings of this present time are not worth comparing with the glory about to be revealed to us. For the creation waits with eager longing for the revealing of the children of God; for the creation was subjected to futility, not of its own will but by the will of the one who subjected it, in hope that the creation itself will be set free from its bondage to decay and will obtain the freedom of the glory of the children of God. We know that the whole creation has been groaning in labor pains until now; and not only the creation, but we ourselves, who have the first fruits of the Spirit, groan inwardly while we wait for adoption, the redemption of our bodies. (Rom 8:18-23)

This reminds us that Christ's resurrection witnesses to us that if we place our trust in him, we too will experience resurrection power in our own lives. We will experience resurrection from all that kills us—whether it is death itself, our sin or the array of our society's systems and structures. But Christ's resurrection is not for us alone. It is, as Paul states so clearly, for all of creation. It is a resurrection of all creation—of society's systems and structures, of the environment, and of us both as individuals and as a community.

Therefore we are more than conquerors at any work to which God may call us, because Christ is in the business of redeeming all of the created order. Our very involvement in ministries that seek to build any portion of humanity into people of power is participation in the resurrection. When we build relationships with people who are in some way oppressed by life, when we work with the powerless, marginalized and exploited to form themselves into people of power, and when we embrace with them the values of a just, equitable and relational culture, we are participating in resurrection power. We are sharing in the resurrection of individuals and their neighborhood, community or city. That is the spirituality of relational power.

You and I, as those empowered by the redeeming power of Jesus Christ, are not called to bring in the kingdom of God, the shalom community. God's intentions for humanity will only be realized fully by God's final intervention in human history. But we are called to be a foretaste of that kingdom, a model of it in our life together, and to work toward God's creation of that shalom community by being involved in

- empowerment of our people as we together confront political systems of oppression and greed
- equitable distribution of wealth so that there will be no poor among us
- relationship with God and each other through Jesus Christ

Only as we commit ourselves to work for shalom community, keeping before ourselves the vision of the world as God intended it to be, can we have a significant impact on the world as it is. That is the Great Commission to which we've been called and the great privilege we have been given as we seek to follow our resurrected Lord and Savior, Jesus Christ, into his world to seek its transformation into God's shalom community.

EPILOGUE
Get On with It!

I AM CURRENTLY AN ACTIVE PARTICIPANT in an effort to organize the relational institutions of the Los Angeles metropolitan area—an urban area so vast that it would fill the states of Connecticut, Massachusetts, Rhode Island and Vermont combined and would still spill over into the Atlantic Ocean! That broad-based organizing effort is named the Los Angeles Metropolitan Organizing Strategy (LA Metro). The basic strategy that we are following to organize an area so large and so diverse is to divide it into geographical clusters. The cluster in which I primarily work is the Pomona Valley, about thirty miles east of the city of Los Angeles and including more than one million people in the cities of Claremont, LaVerne, Montclair, Ontario, Pomona and Upland.

Only institutions that build power through their relationships can join LA Metro, like churches, congregations, mission agencies, parent-teacher organizations, schools and unions. Consequently, I participate in LA Metro through the involvement of the church at which I am parish associate—LaVerne Heights Presbyterian Church. A parish associate is a ministry position in a local congregation of the Presbyterian Church (USA) that is filled by a retired clergyperson or one whose primary ministry is not in a local church. My clergy assignment as parish associate is to provide leadership to our church's involvement in the LA Metro organizing effort.

LaVerne Heights Church is an evangelical congregation of about 260 members who are primarily middle-class, middle-management, Anglo

Christians. This congregation has been very intentional over the years both in the spiritual formation of its members and in its outreach to the world. But participation in the LA Metro organizing effort has given us a window of opportunity both as a congregation and as individual members to work powerfully in the Pomona Valley and throughout the entire Los Angeles metropolis in ways we could not have imagined earlier.

Involvement in the organizing effort has brought the church into a working relationship with churches, organizations and people that this congregation would normally never encounter. Thus members of the church gather monthly with primarily evangelical and Pentecostal churches throughout the Pomona Valley to pray for its cities. Members serve on valleywide action teams on education, health care, housing and homelessness, and youth and senior concerns. There they work in league with members of Roman Catholic, mainline Protestant, evangelical and Pentecostal churches, parent-teacher associations, schools and unions to powerfully address community-wide issues and concerns. These efforts have led to such victories as the overwhelming passage of a citizens' referendum to increase our own taxes in order to keep needed trauma centers from closing; the creation, with school boards, of a program that involves parent participation in the school systems' decision-making processes; and even the convincing of a county supervisor to walk the streets with us and hold individual meetings with her constituency.

But the organizing effort has made a difference to the internal strengthening of LaVerne Heights Church as well. A ministry group of twelve church leaders has formed to provide guidance to the organizing effort in the church. In the past year, these leaders have conducted more than one hundred individual meetings of our parishioners. Eight house meetings have been held. The congregation has enthusiastically received educational events. The principles of community organizing are being applied to both the life of the congregation and the way it organizes itself. (It has done away with committees!) And the congregation is increasingly perceived as an empowered community working for the transformation of the Pomona Valley and the Los Angeles metropolis.

If all this can be true of this church and community, it can be true of yours as well.

One of my favorite verses is Acts 1:11. The followers of the risen Jesus have gathered with him for the last time, and he has commissioned them to "be [his] witnesses in Jerusalem, in all Judea and Samaria, and to the ends of the earth" (Acts 1:8). Suddenly, before their very eyes, Jesus is taken up into heaven. Then comes my favorite part: "Two men in white robes" suddenly appear and say to the disciples, standing there with mouths wide open in utter amazement at what they have just seen, "Men of Galilee, why do you stand looking up toward heaven? This Jesus, who has been taken up from you into heaven, will come in the same way as you saw him go into heaven" (Acts 1:11).

In other words, they are saying to the disciples, "Why are you standing around, gawking? You saw Jesus ascend into heaven. Well, God will bring him back when he is ready. Meanwhile, don't stand around in awe. Get on with it! Get on with the mission of world transformation to which you are called. And God will take care of the rest!"

You've taken the time to read this book, to examine the biblical foundations for a theology of power and to learn some of the essential principles, strategies and tactics for working for the transformation of your world. Now it's time to put the book down and get to work. Get on with the task of working to transform the world into God's intentions for it, because, after all, God has given to you and to your brothers and sisters transforming power that can make the most significant differences in your church and community— if only you will choose to use it!

APPENDIX A
Organizing Networks

There are community, church-based and broad-based organizations in 133 cities of the United States and in several other nations. Most of these local, citywide and metropolitan-wide organizations are a part of one of the organizing networks listed below. Each of these networks provides support and resources to its community organizations, including training events, research, evaluation and trained organizers. Each network, however, has its own distinctive. ACORN organizes individuals rather than institutions. DART organizes in the South and Midwest. Gamaliel has concentrated its organizing in the Midwest. The IAF is the oldest and largest network and concentrates on broad-based organizing. NTIC focuses on providing training, research and technical assistance. PICO began its organizing in western states but has since become national in focus. RCNO organizes especially among small to medium-size African American congregations. Each network regularly holds major three- to ten-day national training workshops for lay people in order to improve their skills and to strengthen their knowledge of organizing. Further information is available on each network on the Web at <www.p-u-t.org> and at the networks' respective websites.

ACORN (Association of Communities Organized for Reform Now)
88 Third Avenue
Brooklyn, NY 11217
Phone: (718) 246-7900
www.acorn.org
Steve Kest, Executive Director

Direct Action and Research Training (DART)
P.O. Box 370791
314 NE 26th Terrace
Miami, FL 33137-0791
Phone: (305) 576-8020
www.thedartcenter.org
John Caulkins, Director

Gamaliel Foundation
203 North Wabash, Suite 808
Chicago, IL 60601
Phone: (312) 357-2639
www.gamaliel.org
Greg Galluzzo, Director

Industrial Areas Foundation (IAF)
220 West Kinzie Street
Chicago, IL 60610
Phone: (312) 245-9211
(For Web information on IAF, go to www.p-u-t.org and click on "Organizing Networks.")
Edward T. Chambers, Executive Director

National Training and Information Center
810 N. Milwaukee Avenue
Chicago, IL 60622
Phone: (312) 243-3035
www.ntic-us.org
Gail Cincotta, Executive Director

Pacific Institute for Community Organization (PICO)
171 Santa Rosa Avenue
Oakland, CA 94610
Phone: (510) 655-2801
www.piconetwork.org
Ed Bauman, Executive Director

Regional Congregations and Neighborhood Organizations (RCNO)
738 East 92nd Street
Los Angeles, CA 90002
Phone: (323) 755-RCNO
www.rcno.org (This website is under construction; for information on RCNO, go to www.p-u-t.org and click on "Organizing Networks.")
Eugene Williams, Director

APPENDIX B
Written and Video Resources

The bibliography lists some of the best books on community organizing. Following is a list of other resources available on video and on the printed page that can help a congregation or Christian organization both develop a theology of power and organizing and learn some strategies. These resources are available from Partners in Urban Transformation, Mailbox #44, 25101 Bear Valley Road, Tehachapi, CA 93561-8311; phone: (661) 821-0656; e-mail: PUTOffice@surfbest.net; website: <www.p-u-t.org >.

Building a People of Power—This resource is a twenty-seven-session course on a theology and practice of power taught by Robert Linthicum, Marilyn Stranske and Mike Miller. Each session is ninety minutes in length. The course is used in training programs of Youth With A Mission and World Vision International. It is also used at a graduate level in academic institutions throughout the United States and by a number of churches, denominations and mission agencies. Designed for both individual distance learning and small-group learning, the course can be taken for graduate academic credit. The resource consists of fourteen instructional videotapes, a student's workbook, a facilitator's handbook and a textbook. Detailed information on this video course is available on the website of Partners in Urban Transformation, <www.p-u-t.org >.

City of God; City of Satan: A Biblical Theology of the Urban Church—This award-winning book by Robert Linthicum develops a biblical theology of the city, along with a philosophy of and strategies for urban ministry and the building of a spirituality equal to the demands of ministry in the mission field of the world city. It has been translated into Chinese, Korean, Portuguese and Spanish and has been distributed throughout the world. It was the bestselling religious book in Brazil in 1993.

Empowering the Poor—This textbook on community and broad-based organizing presents strategies for effective urban ministry that truly empower the people with whom you are ministering rather than making them dependent on your intervention. "If you are going to read just one book on urban ministry, this is the book to read," wrote Stu Imbach of the Overseas Mission Fellowship.

NOTES

Chapter 1: Society as God Intended It to Be

[1]All statistics on the Hollywood-Wilshire community were compiled from a study done for the Cluster by Percept, a research and resource business that works primarily with churches and denominations. The study was based on information from the U.S. Census Bureau, the City of Los Angeles, the Los Angeles Unified School District and several commercial studies.

[2]This story was first published in Robert Linthicum, *City of God; City of Satan: A Biblical Theology of the Urban Church* (Grand Rapids, Mich.: Zondervan, 1991), pp. 45-46.

[3]"Strangers and Gentiles," *Encyclopedia Judaica,* vol. 15 (Jerusalem: Encyclopedia Judaica, 1971), pp. 419-21; Moses Maimonides, *Mishneh Torah,* Hilkhot Issurei Biah 14:7-8; *Shulhan Arukh,* Yoreh Deah 124:2; Raphael Juspe, "Sabbath, Sabbatical and Jubilee: Jewish Ethical Perspectives," *The Jubilee Challenge: Utopia or Possibility?* (Geneva, Switzerland: WCC, 1997), pp. 87-90.

[4]Jesus reiterated this when he said, "You always have the poor with you" (Mt 26:11; compare Deut 15:11). Those who wish to justify an increasing division of the impoverished and the wealthy often use this statement. But to do so is to significantly misuse Scripture. Jesus quoted Deuteronomy within the context of the reality that he would not always be with Israel. It is illegitimate eisegesis to use Jesus' quotation of Deuteronomy 15:11 as a means to justify both poverty and a nation doing nothing to eliminate it.

[5]Materials on shalom were taken from Jack L. Stotts, *Shalom: the Search for a Peaceable City* (Nashville: Abingdon, 1973); C. F. Evans, "Peace," *A Theological Wordbook of the Bible,* ed. Alan Richardson (New York: Macmillan, 1960), pp. 165-66; E. M. Good, "Peace in the Old Testament," *The Interpreter's Dictionary of the Bible,* ed. George Arthur Buttrick (New York: Abingdon, 1962), 4:704-6; and C. L. Mitton, "Peace in the New Testament," *The Interpreter's Dictionary of the Bible,* ed. George Arthur Buttrick (New York: Abingdon, 1962), 4:704-6.

[6]Gen 1:26—3:8; Ex 21:5; Lev 19:18-34; 25:8-46; 1 Kings 5:1; Ps 48, 72, 122, 125, 132; Prov 10:12; 14:21; 17:9; 31:1-31; Is 2:2-4; 65:19-25; Mic 6:1-8; Mt 13:31-33; 25:31-46; Lk 6:20-26; 17:20-21; 18:18-30; Eph 1:20-23; 3:1-21; Col 1:3-29; Rev 17—18 (for the image of a thoroughly corrupt society), 21—22 (for the image of a society as God intended it to be).

[7]Roland H. Bainton, *Christendom: A Short History of Christianity and Its Impact on Western Civilization* (New York: Harper & Row, 1966), pp. 136-39; Earle E. Cairns, *Christianity Through the Centuries* (Grand Rapids, Mich.: Zondervan, 1954), pp. 166-68; Kenneth Scott Latourette,

A History of Christianity (New York: Harper & Brothers, 1953), pp. 333-36; Williston Walker, *A History of the Christian Church,* 3rd ed. (New York: Charles Scribner's Sons, 1970), pp. 127-28. A shortened compendium of *The Rule of St. Benedict* is found in Henry Bettenson, *Documents of the Christian Church* (London: Oxford University Press, 1943), pp. 164-81.

Chapter 2: What Keeps Going Wrong?

[1]From 900 B.C. through 586 B.C., the Israelite empire of David and Solomon was divided into two competing nations: Israel (also known as the Northern Kingdom) and Judah (the Southern Kingdom). By Ezekiel's time, the Northern Kingdom had been destroyed by Assyria in 722-1 B.C. Therefore Ezekiel's prophecies were directed to Judah. Because Judah was all that remained of the larger Israel, I will follow Ezekiel's lead and call it "Israel."

[2]Ichiro Kawachi and Bruce P. Kennedy, *The Health of Nations* (New York: New Press, 2002), pp. 77-82.

[3]Ibid., p. 112.

[4]Paul Krugman, "For Richer: How the Permissive Capitalism of the Boom Destroyed American Equality," *New York Times Magazine,* October 20, 2002, pp. 64-65.

[5]Kawachi and Kennedy, *Health of Nations,* p. 171.

[6]It is important to note that Ezekiel didn't end his prophecy on such a pessimistic note. The final chapters of Ezekiel tell about the rebuilding of Jerusalem as the restored Deuteronomic city. And the final words of the book are, "The name of the city from that time on shall be, The LORD is There" (Ezek 48:35). The *shekinah* had returned.

Chapter 3: What Was Jesus About?

[1]André Trocmé, *Jesus and the Nonviolent Revolution* (Eugene, Ore.: Wipf & Stock, 1998), p. 87.

[2]Ibid., p. 54.

[3]Donald B. Kraybill, *The Upside-Down Kingdom* (Scottdale, Pa.: Herald, 1990), pp. 47-48.

[4]Trocmé, *Jesus and the Nonviolent Revolution,* p. 54.

[5]Ibid., p. 56.

[6]Ibid., pp. 93-94.

[7]Ched Myers, *Binding the Strong Man: A Political Reading of Mark's Story of Jesus* (Maryknoll, N.Y.: Orbis, 1988), pp. 75-76; Kraybill, *Upside-Down Kingdom,* pp. 68-69.

[8]Kraybill, *Upside-Down Kingdom,* pp. 61-65; Myers, *Binding the Strong Man,* pp. 49, 78-80; Trocmé, *Jesus and the Nonviolent Revolution,* pp. 73, 89.

[9]William R. Herzog II, *Parables as Subversive Speech: Jesus as Pedagogue of the Oppressed* (Louisville: Westminster John Knox, 1994), pp. 58-63; Kraybill, *Upside-Down Kingdom,* pp. 75-78.

[10]Kraybill, *Upside-Down Kingdom,* pp. 78-82; Trocmé, *Jesus and the Nonviolent Revolution,* pp. 86-88.

[11]Herzog, *Parables as Subversive Speech,* pp. 63-66; Myers, *Binding the Strong Man,* pp. 48-53.

[12]Considerable research has now been accumulated on Jewish and other agrarian cultures of the Mediterranean and Near Eastern worlds of the centuries surrounding the time of Jesus. Such research places an unparalleled understanding of both the ministry of Jesus and the writings of the four Gospels into a social, political, economic and religious context. Seminal research that now informs such biblical social analysis includes Walter Brueggemann, *The*

Prophetic Imagination (Philadelphia: Fortress, 1978); Thomas F. Carney, *The Shape of the Past: Models and Antiquity* (Lawrence, Kans.: Coronado, 1975); Shmuel Noah Eisenstadt, *The Political Systems of Empires* (New York: Free Press, 1963), and with L. Roniger, *Patrons, Clients and Friends: Interpersonal Relations and the Structure of Trust in Society* (Cambridge: Cambridge University Press, 1984); John Kautsky, *The Politics of Aristocratic Empires* (Chapel Hill: University of North Carolina Press, 1982); Gerhard E. Lenski, *Power and Privilege: A Theory of Social Stratification* (New York: McGraw-Hill, 1966), and with Jean Lenski, *Human Societies: An Introduction to Macrosociology*, 4th ed. (New York: McGraw-Hill, 1982); Bruce Malina, *The New Testament World: Insights from Cultural Anthropology* (Atlanta: John Knox Press, 1981), and with Richard Rohrbaugh, *Social-Science Commentary on the Synoptic Gospels* (Minneapolis: Fortress, 1992); Halvor Moxnes, *The Economy of the Kingdom: Social Conflict and Economic Relations in Luke's Gospel* (Philadelphia: Fortress, 1988); Jacob Neusner et al., *The Social World of Formative Christianity and Judaism* (Leiden: E. J. Brill, 1988); Douglas Oakman, "Jesus and Agrarian Palestine: The Factor of Debt," Society of Biblical Literature Seminar Papers, 24:57-73, 1985; Trocmé, *Jesus and the Nonviolent Revolution*; Walter Wink, *Engaging the Powers: Discernment and Resistance in a World of Domination* (Minneapolis: Fortress, 1992), and *The Powers That Be: Theology for a New Millennium* (New York: Doubleday, 1998).

[13]The relationship of the stories about rich men in Luke was developed by Mark Allan Powell, professor of New Testament at Trinity Lutheran Seminary, Columbus, Ohio, and is used by permission.

[14]Dietrich Bonhoeffer, *Life Together* (New York: Harper & Row, 1954), p. 8.

[15]Kraybill, *Upside-Down Kingdom*, p. 125.

[16]For a more thorough study of the intent of each of the Gospel writers, view sessions 6—9 of the video course *Building a People of Power* by Robert Linthicum (Colorado Springs: Crown, 2000). The video can be obtained from Partners in Urban Transformation, Mailbox #44, 25101 Bear Valley Road, Tehachapi, CA 93561-8311; (661) 821-0656; <www.p-u-t.org >. Other helpful works are listed in endnotes 1, 3, 7, 9, 12, 18 and 19.

[17]Paul Hertig, "The Multi-Ethnic Journeys of Jesus in Matthew: Margin-Center Dynamics," *Missiology: An International Review* 25, no. 1 (1998): 23-35.

[18]Athol Gill, *Life On the Road: The Gospel Basis for a Messianic Lifestyle* (Homebush, Australia: Lancer, 1989); Ched Myers, *Binding the Strong Man*.

[19]Wes Howard-Brook, *Becoming Children of God: John's Gospel and Radical Discipleship* (Maryknoll, N.Y.: Orbis, 1994).

Chapter 4: What Should the Church Be About?

[1]The Hebrew word is *galah;* that word contains within it the components of "exile" (that is, forced removal from the land) and of "going forth," "emigrating" or "being sent"; see Francis Brown, S. R. Driver and Charles A. Briggs, *Hebrew and English Lexicon of the Old Testament* (Oxford: Oxford University Press, 1959), pp.162-63.

[2]John Bright, *The Anchor Bible*, vol. 21, *Jeremiah* (Garden City, N.Y.: Doubleday, 1965), p. 211.

[3]See Jack Stotts, *Shalom: The Search for a Peaceable City* (Nashville: Abingdon, 1973); E. M. Good, "Peace in the Old Tesament," *The Interpreter's Dictionary of the Bible,* ed. George Arthur Buttrick (New York: Abingdon, 1962); C. L. Mitton, "Peace in the New Testament," *The In-*

terpreter's Dictionary of the Bible, ed. George Arthur Buttrick (New York: Abingdon, 1962); Wes Howard-Brook, *Becoming Children of God: John's Gospel and Radical Discipleship* (Maryknoll, N.Y.: Orbis, 1994), pp. 456-59; and Brown, Driver and Brigg's *Hebrew and English Lexicon of the Old Testament.*

[4]From the New International Version, the Living Bible, the New Revised Standard Version and the Jerusalem Bible.

[5]"Redlining" is the illegal practice of withholding home-loan funds or insurance or to otherwise discriminate against people who live in neighborhoods considered high economic risks. To redline a community is to initiate an action that, if not stopped, will inevitably bring about decline in the neighborhood's housing (because people can't get loans to purchase, repair, renovate or protect their property from calamity), resulting in decay and eventual collapse of the community.

[6]I am indebted to the Industrial Areas Foundation (IAF) and particularly its formulation of power as found in the teachings of Ernesto Cortes, Sister Maribeth Larkin and Sister Christine Stephens in the IAF ten-day training given on July 7-16, 1998.

[7]I heard the expression "Acting yourself into a new way of thinking" for the first time from Don McClanen, founder of both the Ministry of Money and the Fellowship of Christian Athletes. I am grateful to him for this profound statement of how human beings change.

Chapter 5: Nehemiah and the Iron Rule of Power

[1]Martin Buber, *Ten Rungs: Hasidic Sayings* (New York: Schocken, 1947), p. 84.

[2]In Nehemiah 2:10 it is unclear if Sanballat and Tobiah had heard of Nehemiah's journey to Jerusalem and its purpose from secondary sources or if Nehemiah had visited them directly. The latter makes the most sense, because it would have been proper protocol for Nehemiah to make at least a courtesy visit to the governor of the province where he would be on assignment from the emperor. And such a visit would have given Nehemiah opportunity to determine whether Sanballat would be cooperative or resistant.

[3]The book of Nehemiah is divided into two parts. Chapters one through six deal with Israel organizing to address its most immediate problem—their broken-down walls and sense of vulnerability. Chapters seven through thirteen deal with Israel organizing to address its deepest spiritual problem—the broken-down corporate life and the need to embrace the Deuteronomic covenant.

[4]Mark R. Warren and Richard L. Wood, *Faith-Based Community Organizing: The State of the Field* (New York: Interfaith Funders, 2001), pp. 5-6.

[5]I am indebted to the Reverend Dennis A. Davis for these insights, as presented in a paper for a course I was teaching. The paper was "Organizing Principles That Affect Ways to Go About Providing Leadership to a Church or Christian Organization" and is used by permission.

[6]The second half of the book of Nehemiah (chaps. 7—13) records the rebuilding of the corporate life of Israel. We will not deal with that social transformation in this book, but that analysis is developed fully in my book *Building a People of Power,* chap. 16, "We're Here Because He Was There: Nehemiah and the Transformation of Society" (to be released in 2005). A draft of this chapter is available for a nominal fee from Partners in Urban Transformation, Mailbox #44, 25101 Bear Valley Road, Tehachapi, CA 93561-8311; (661) 821-0656, <www.p-u-t.org>.

[7]It is important to clearly identify the process Nehemiah used to discern the issue and to initiate action to substantively address that issue. There is no evidence from the text that he saw the broken-down walls of Jerusalem as the organizing issue until the Jews visiting Susa identified it as such (Neh 1:3). In fact he rightly identified Israel's true issue as being a spiritual and cultural problem (Neh 1:5-7). But as one who thoroughly understood power (an inevitable attribute of anyone who is servant to a king), Nehemiah recognized the potential for organizing the people around the challenge of rebuilding of the walls. Therefore he took them through a process of reflection similar to what he himself had followed (Neh 2:17-19), so that, like him, they concluded that rebuilding the walls was the first action step they needed to take. But in the final analysis, the decision had to be theirs to make, for without them making that decision, it would have been impossible to succeed in completing the task (as implied in Neh 5:1-6).

Chapter 6: Jesus Is Caesar

[1]The New Testament theologian who has made the most exhaustive study of this subject and is most influential in present New Testament studies on the first-century understanding of principalities and powers is scholar Walter Wink. Notable is *The Powers,* his exhaustive three-volume study of first-century Christian, Jewish, Greek and Roman understandings of the links between the spiritual and earthly dimensions of life and of the systems. The three books are *Engaging the Powers* (Fortress, 1992), *Naming the Powers* (1984) and *Unmasking the Powers* (1986). See also his synopsis of the study *The Powers That Be* (Doubleday, 1998).

[2]There has been considerable debate among biblical scholars since the nineteenth century as to whether Paul is the author of Ephesians or not, with weighty evidence on both sides of the argument. Most notable among the arguments against Pauline authorship is the profoundly different style of writing than that of his unquestionably authentic letters. The strongest argument in favor of Pauline authorship is the tradition of the church for that authorship that stretches back to the century after its initial publication. I hold to the Pauline authorship of the epistle, both on theological grounds and because I don't believe the evidence against such authorship is sufficient to require me to change my position. Consequently, throughout this chapter, I will refer to Paul as the author of Ephesians.

[3]The distorted translation first appeared in the original King James Version of the Bible and was passed down into both subsequent KJV editions and into other translations. The Greek language has two words that are normally translated "to"—one that means "in order to" and the other that means "so to" or "so that." The way those two Greek words are used by Paul in Ephesians 4:12 requires the translation to read "to equip the saints in order to do their work of ministry, so that the body of Christ can be built up." It is important to keep in mind that when the KJV was first translated, the church was very concerned about securing the office and the exclusive work of the clergy in light of the uncertainty the Reformation in England had brought that office. By translating this passage so it would appear that there was a threefold responsibility for the clergy (that is, to teach [equip], to do pastoral care [the work of ministry] and to strengthen the church), this would—and did—strengthen the office of the clergy in English society. But the Greek text will not support such a translation, no matter the motives of the translator. The accurate translation of Ephesians 4:12 is given in the NRSV, the NIV, the NLT and the Jerusalem Bible and is corrected in the NKJV.

Chapter 7: Building Power Around Relationships

[1]The argument presented in its entirety that Nehemiah was a key factor in the development of Judaism is developed in my paper "We're Here Because He Was There: Nehemiah and the Transformation of Society" (Paper 011). Paper 011 can be ordered (either electronically or in hard copy) for a nominal fee from Partners in Urban Transformation, Mailbox #44, 25101 Bear Valley Road, Tehachapi, CA 93561-8311; e-mail: putoffice@surfbest.net; website: <www.p-u-t.org>.

[2]Some of the material presented on the conduct of an individual meeting contains principles presented by Marilyn Stranske in her paper "The Individual Meeting: A Way of Life and Ministry," in the Student Workbook of the video course *Building a People of Power* (Colorado Springs: Crown, 2000), pp. 41-43. This paper (Paper 012) is also available from Partners in Urban Transformation.

[3]For a detailed description and analysis of these informal leadership roles, see my book *Empowering the Poor* (Monrovia, Calif.: MARC Publications, 1991), pp. 48-51.

[4]A template already created for the storage and retrieval of data can be purchased from Partners in Urban Transformation for a nominal fee. The Individual Meetings Template is available in both Microsoft Access XP and Microsoft Excel XP. For further information contact Partners in Urban Transformation.

Chapter 8: Organizing for Community Action

[1]The male disciples were Simon Peter, Andrew, James and John (both sons of Zebedee), Philip, Bartholomew, Thomas, Matthew, James Alphaeus, Thaddaeus, Simon the Zealot, and Judas Iscariot (Mt 10:1-4). The seven female disciples were Mary Magdalene (Lk 8:3); Mary and Martha, sisters of Lazarus (Lk 10:38-41; Jn 11:1-44); Joanna (Lk 8:3; 24:10); Susanna (Lk 8:3); Salome (Mk 15:40; 16:1); and Mary the mother of James (Lk 24:10). There was also a Mary the wife of Clopas listed (Jn 19:25), but I assume she is also the mother of James; if not, that means there were eight female disciples.

[2]The vocabulary of community and broad-based organizing uses the word *target* for the specific official whom the organization selects to receive the issue and to act upon it. *Target* is intentionally used because he or she is the person "targeted" to respond to the demands of the organization. Normally the target is that person in a government, public organization or business who has the authority to make the decision required by the community organization. Why use the word *target* for that person? Simply because to use the word *enemy* or any other pejorative is to create a condition that could lead to a permanent division between the community organization and that person. One doesn't want to allow such alienation to occur, because the target may become the community organization's supporter on another issue. This nuance is captured in the organizing expression "There are no permanent friends or enemies!"

[3]The word *action* is another technical term in the field of organizing. An action is an intentional and deliberate act on the part of the organization to require the response of a target on the issue that the organization has determined necessary to act on.

[4]Most community and broad-based organizations operate on the understanding that each member church and institution makes a decision whether or not to participate in each issue. The organization does this out of sensitivity to the potential differences between churches and

institutions. The basic assumption is that each member institution participates as much as possible in each issue proposed by each action team, but no institution is expected to participate when this would go against the convictions or priorities of that institution.

[5]There is little written on the application of organizing principles to the interior life and institutional development of the local church. However, my book *Building a Church of Power*, scheduled for release late in 2004 or early in 2005, will concentrate on this theme.

Chapter 9: Biblical Tactics for Change Avoided by Today's Church

[1]The name of Madras has now been changed by the government of India to Chennai, but at the time of this story, it was named Madras, so I will use that name.

[2]Excerpted from a larger article written by Robert Linthicum, "Doing Community Organizing in the Urban Slums of India," *Social Policy* 32, no. 2 (winter 2001-2002): 34-38. Used by permission.

Chapter 10: The Spirituality of Relational Power

[1]There is a significant body of work on the development of leadership within the context of community organizing, including Gregory F. A. Pierce, *Activism That Makes Sense: Congregations and Community Organization* (Chicago: ACTA Publications, 1984), chap. 7; Samuel Freedman, *Upon This Rock: The Miracles of a Black Church* (New York: HarperCollins, 1993); Paulo Friere, *Pedagogy of the Oppressed,* trans. Myra Bergman Ramos (New York: Herder & Herder, 1972); "Biblical Examples and Principles in Team Building," a chapter I wrote on leadership development from an organizing perspective in *Leadership and Team Building: Transforming Congregational Ministry through Teams,* ed. Roger Heuser (Matthews, N.C.: Institute of Church Leadership, Christian Ministry Resources, 1999), pp. 226-49. Also see my book *Empowering the Poor* (Monrovia, Calif.: MARC Publications, 1991), chap. 7, pp. 61-68 (a chapter on the pedagogy of action and reflection—the primary teaching philosophy for community and broad-based organizing and the building of leaders).

[2]A thorough exploration of the formation of values and spirituality in community organizing is found in the video course *Building a People of Power*, sessions 26 and 27. The video course can be obtained from Partners in Urban Transformation, Mailbox #44, 25101 Bear Valley Road, Tehachapi, CA 93561-8311; phone: (661) 821-0656; e-mail: PUTOffice@surfbest.net.

[3]Ichiro Kawachi and Bruce P. Kennedy, *The Health of Nations* (New York: New Press, 2002), pp. 15-18.

BIBLIOGRAPHY

BIBLICAL THEOLOGY OF POWER

Bakke, Ray. *A Theology as Big as the City.* Downers Grove, Ill.: InterVarsity Press, 1997.

Brueggemann, Walter. *Hopeful Imagination: Prophetic Vision in Exile.* Philadelphia: Fortress, 1986.

————. *The Prophetic Imagination.* Philadelphia: Fortress, 1978.

Elliott, Charles. *Praying the Kingdom: Towards a Political Spirituality.* New York: Paulist, 1985.

Howard-Brook, Wes. *Becoming Children of God: John's Gospel and Radical Discipleship.* Maryknoll, N.Y.: Orbis, 1994.

Kinsler, Ross, and Gloria Kinsler. *The Biblical Jubilee and the Struggle for Life.* Maryknoll, N.Y.: Orbis, 1999.

Kraybill, Donald B. *The Upside-Down Kingdom.* Scottdale, Pa.: Herald, 1978.

Linthicum, Robert C. *City of God; City of Satan: A Biblical Theology of the Urban Church.* Grand Rapids, Mich.: Zondervan, 1991.

Meeks, Wayne A. *The First Urban Christians: The Social World of the Apostle Paul.* New Haven, Conn.: Yale University Press, 1983.

Myers, Ched. *Binding the Strong Man: A Political Reading of Mark's Story of Jesus.* Maryknoll, N.Y.: Orbis, 1988.

Trocmé, André. *Jesus and the Nonviolent Revolution.* Eugene, Ore.: Wipf & Stock, 1998.

Ucko, Hans, ed. *The Jubilee Challenge: Utopia or Possibility.* Geneva, Switzerland: WCC Publications, 1997.

Wink, Walter. *Engaging the Powers: Discernment and Resistance in a World of Domination.* Minneapolis: Augsburg Fortress, 1992.

————. *The Powers That Be: Theology for a New Millennium.* New York: Doubleday, 1998.

COMMUNITY AND BROAD-BASED ORGANIZING

Alinsky, Saul D. *Reveille for Radicals.* New York: Vintage, 1980.

———. *Rules for Radicals.* New York: Vintage, 1972.

Bobo, Kim, Jackie Kendall and Steve Max. *Organizing for Social Change: A Manual for Activists.* Seven Lock, 1991.

Friere, Paulo. *Pedagogy of the Oppressed.* Translated by Myra Bergman Ramos. 1970; reprint, New York: Continuum, 1986.

Grecan, Michael. *Going Public.* New York: Beacon, 2002.

Horwitt, Sanford. *Let Them Call Me Rebel: Saul Alinsky—His Life and Legacy.* New York: Alfred Knopf, 1981.

Linthicum, Robert, Mike Miller and Marilyn Stranske. *Building a People of Power: A Workbook and Urban Reader.* Colorado Springs: Crown, 2000.

———. *Empowering the Poor: Community Organizing Among the City's "Rag, Tag and Bobtail."* 2nd ed. Monrovia, Calif.: MARC Publications, 1999.

Pierce, Gregory F. A. *Activism That Makes Sense: Congregations and Community Organization.* Chicago: ACTA Publications, 1984.

Rogers, Mary Beth. *Cold Anger: A Story of Faith and Power Politics.* Denton: University of North Texas Press, 1990.

Roy, Arundhati. *Power Politics.* Cambridge, Mass.: South End, 2001.

Warren, Mark R. *Dry Bones Rattling: Community Building to Revitalize American Democracy.* Princeton, N.J.: Princeton University Press, 2001.

MINISTRY AND ECCLESIOLOGY

Bakke, Ray, and Sam Roberts. *The Expanded Mission of City Churches.* Chicago: International Urban Associates, 1998.

Branch, Taylor. *Parting the Waters: America in the King Years 1954-63.* New York: Simon & Schuster, 1988.

Conn, Harvie M. *A Clarified Vision for Urban Mission.* Grand Rapids, Mich.: Zondervan, 1987.

Dulles, Avery. *Models of the Church.* New York: Image, 1978.

Freedman, Samuel G. *Upon This Rock: The Miracle of a Black Church.* New York: Simon & Collins, 1993.

Guder, Darrell. *Missional Church.* Grand Rapids, Mich.: Eerdmans, 1998.

Hertig, Young Lee. *Cultural Tug of War: The Korean Immigrant Family and Church in Transition.* Nashville: Abingdon, 2001.

Kim, Young-Il, ed. *Knowledge, Attitude and Experience: Ministry in the Cross-Cultural Context.* Nashville, Abingdon, 1992.

Kunjufu, Jawanza. *Black Economics: Solutions for Economic and Community Empower-*

206

ment. Chicago: African American Image, 1991.

Newbigin, Lesslie. *The Gospel in a Pluralistic Society.* Grand Rapids, Mich.: Eerdmans, 1989.

Ortiz, Manuel. *The Hispanic Challenge: Opportunities Confronting the Church.* Downers Grove, Ill.: InterVarsity Press, 1993.

Regele, Mike. *Death of the Church.* Grand Rapids, Mich.: Zondervan, 1995.

Sample, Tex. *Blue Collar Ministry: Facing Economic and Social Realities of Working People.* Philadelphia: Judson Press, 1987.

————. *U.S. Lifestyles and Mainline Churches: A Key to Reaching People in the 90's.* Louisville: Westminster Press, 1990.

Schaller, Lyle E. *Center City Churches: the New Urban Frontier.* Nashville: Abingdon, 1993.

Smith, Donald P. *Congregations Alive: Practical Suggestions for Bringing Your Church to Life Through Partnership in Ministry.* Louisville: Westminster Press, 1981.

Tillapaugh, Frank R. *Unleashing the Church: Getting People Out of the Fortress and Into Ministry.* Ventura, Calif.: Regal, 1982.

Villafañe, Eldin. *Seek the Peace of the City: Reflections on Urban Ministry.* Grand Rapids, Mich.: Eerdmans, 1995.

Williams, Cecil. *No Hiding Place: Empowerment and Recovery of Our Troubled Communities.* New York: Harper & Row, 1992.

Yamamori, Tetsunao, Bryant L. Myers and Kenneth L. Luscombe. *Serving with the Urban Poor.* Monrovia, Calif.: MARC Publications, 1998.

Younger, George D. *From New Creation to Urban Crisis: A History of Action Training Ministries 1962-1975.* Chicago: Center for the Scientific Study of Religion, 1987.

Urbanism and Urbanization

Dogan, Mattei, and John D. Kasarda. *Mega-Cities: The Metropolis Era.* Beverly Hills, Calif.: Sage Foundation, 1988.

————. *A World of Giant Cities.* Beverly Hills, Calif.: Sage Foundation, 1988.

Fluker, Walter E. *They Look For a City: A Comparative Analysis of the Ideal Community in the Thought of Howard Thurman and Martin Luther King Jr.* Lanham, Md.: University Press of America, 1989.

Fulton, William. *The Reluctant Metropolis: The Politics of Urban Growth in Los Angeles.* Point Arena, Calif.: Solano, 1997.

Gibbs, Jewell Taylor. *Young, Black and Male in America: An Endangered Species.* Dover, Mass.: Auburn House, 1988.

Jacobs, Jane. *Cities and the Wealth of Nations.* New York: Random House, 1984.

Mumford, Lewis. *The City in History: Its Origins, Its Transformations, and Its Prospects.*

New York: Harcourt Brace Jovanovich, 1961.

Palen, J. John. *The Urban World.* 2nd ed. New York: McGraw-Hill, 1981.

Sassen, Saskia. *The Global City.* Princeton, N.J.: Princeton University Press, 1991.

Wallerstein, Immanuel. *Utopistics: Historical Choices of the Twenty-First Century.* New York: New Press, 1998.

Subject Index